Thor

Happy Birthday

1989

Dad

HOW TO SHOOT

HOW TO SHOOT

A COMPLETE GUIDE TO THE USE OF SPORTING FIREARMS—
RIFLES, SHOTGUNS, AND HANDGUNS—ON THE RANGE AND
IN THE FIELD

by LARRY KOLLER

with special photography by Everette Short

NEW REVISED EDITION
edited by Robert Elman, Russ Carpenter and Steve Ferber

DOUBLEDAY & COMPANY, INC., GARDEN CITY, NEW YORK

Acknowledgment is due to the following sources for pictures in this book.

Winchester News Bureau: pages 36, 63, 76 top, 91, 92 bottom, 99 bottom, 111, 128, 195, 197. Official Marine Corps Photo, page 54 bottom. Photos on pages 102 through 108 posed by Dick Gordon, Class AA skeet shooter, co-owner of the Thunder Mountain Winchester Gun Club, Ringwood, N.J.; these photographs were taken by the author. Gaines Dog Research: page 114. New Brunswick Travel Bureau: pages 115, 116. Ontario Department of Lands and Forests, pages 121, 123. Florida Development Commission, page 122. Robert Elman, page 130 top right. Federal Bureau of Investigation, page 149. Steve Ferber, page 157. National Rifle Association, page 158. Arkansas Game & Fish Commission, page 189. U. S. Fish and Wildlife Service, pages 190, 194. U. S. Forest Service, page 191. Russ Carpenter, page 231.

To Paul,
my youngest son,
who modeled for most of
the pictures in this book—
sometimes unwillingly—
but nevertheless professionally

CONTENTS

INTRODUCTION

We have been a country of hunters and outdoorsmen since the days of our first pioneers; skill with firearms is a tradition in our nation. Over 16,000,000 hunters buy licenses each year and millions more shoot at paper bull's-eyes and clay targets or collect firearms. Each year, at least 1,000,000 youngsters come of hunting age.

Those of us who shoot, or who want to shoot, share a responsibility to maintain the tradition of skill—and along with it, safety and sportsmanship that are integral parts of this tradition. The goal of this book is to provide a large measure of this skill. It is a complete course in how to handle all three types of sporting firearms—rifles, shotguns, and handguns—in all sporting situations. And it is designed to help both the novice and the experienced shooter.

For the beginner, it will be an enormously helpful textbook and practical guide, since it emphasizes specific fundamentals on an informal—and, we hope, informative—basis. We stress field shooting rather than the rigid formalities imposed by the target range. These, too, are explained, but the point is that our methods will enable any person of normal physical capabilities to become a good all-around shot in a relatively short time.

Veteran shooters will certainly find some new ideas in these pages. And it does no harm to brush up on old techniques. Furthermore, this approach will help any expert who wishes to instruct others; this volume can be used as a teaching manual, guiding the coach so that he gives his lessons in proper order and leaves nothing out.

It will be best—especially for novices—to read the volume through in order, because it might prove difficult to get a complete understanding of a chapter read out of context. However, if you plan to do a particular kind of shooting one day (skeet, for instance), you will be well advised to reread the appropriate chapter (on clay target shooting, in this case) the night before. You will find that you retain the instructions better this way, and, of course, by putting them to use you will stamp them even more sharply into your memory. Also, if a given shooting position or hold seems foreign to you, try it before going on with your reading. You will find that this makes each process clear and easy.

Bear in mind also that for the sake of simplicity the instructions are given for right-handed shooters. If you are a southpaw, simply switch the directions appropriately.

Most of this book's illustrations were made especially, to clarify the techniques being taught. They are arranged to be more useful if studied as you read the text, not before you read a chapter or after you finish it. By giving them careful attention as you read, you will associate the instructions with graphic demonstrations, making the techniques and sequence of operations clearly understandable. These illustrations cover gun parts as well as gun handling and actual shooting, because a knowledge of firearms construction and function contributes to safety—an important part of this book—as well as to proficiency.

It is vital in learning to shoot that you start with no preconceived notions. Most beginners, and some fairly experienced shooters, don't realize that relaxation is essential, that shooting can and should be as natural as throwing a ball or pointing a finger. A firearm must never be handled as if it were some strange, fearsome machine, but rather as if it were an extension of your hands and body. There is no magic in shooting, and little, if any, luck. Your eyes and hands simply direct the bullet or shot charge to the target, and it's easier than most beginners think.

I have called upon my 40 years of experience in the game fields and on the target ranges to relate my methods of shooting, methods that have been successful not only in raising target scores but in hunting every species of animal and game bird taken with firearms. I have found that no one is so good a shooter that he can't improve by occasionally consulting a reference work. Used in this way, this book will teach you what you need to know—and then help you to remember it.

LARRY KOLLER
Monroe, New York

HOW TO SHOOT

Chapter 1

HOW TO BE SAFE EVERY TIME YOU CARRY A GUN

In shooting, as in most other endeavors, first things come first. And the big first with firearms is safety. This is not to say that guns have a higher degree of potential danger than other mechanical devices such as cars, bathtubs, step-ladders, chain saws, paring knives, and other work-a-day items. It is simply that a firearm has a deadly intent in its design—it is meant for killing.

The beginner handling his first gun is at once awed by the mechanical concept that puts a directable destructive force in his hands and, inevitably, he is as much fascinated by the tradition, legend, and history surrounding the gun as he is by its mechanics. Surprisingly few people, despite a long American heritage in the use of firearms, actually know how a gun works, how the power package represented by the cartridge is tamed and controlled, how the cunningly devised grooves in a rifled barrel are contrived and how they function, how the pressure of a finger on the trigger is transported to fire the gun, and why, even though the gun is a lethal device, it is as harmless as a baseball bat when used with intelligence and care.

Actually, a shooter can handle firearms all his life in complete safety without knowing exactly how they work. But it is a big help if he does know; the old saying that familiarity breeds contempt does not apply to guns. The man who knows most about guns has the most respect for them and handles them properly. In this book, one of our aims is to familiarize the reader with the mechanics and functions of sporting firearms and their ammunition. This familiarity is the basic factor in safe gun handling.

Shooters for many years have been exposed to the "Ten Commandments of Safety." These arc general rules, all-encompassing, and, when strictly adhered to, they assure safe gun handling for the shooter and safety to all persons within range of his firearm. A few of these rules should be examined especially closely.

THE 10 COMMANDMENTS OF SAFETY—COMMON-SENSE RULES EVERY BEGINNER SHOULD LEARN

1. Treat every gun with the respect due a loaded gun. This is the first rule of gun safety.
2. Guns carried into camp or home, or when otherwise not in use, must always be unloaded and taken down or have actions open; guns always should be carried in cases to the shooting area.
3. Always be sure barrel and action are clear of obstructions and that you have only ammunition of the proper size for the gun you are carrying. Remove oil and grease from chamber before firing.
4. Always carry your gun so that you can control the direction of the muzzle even if you stumble; keep the safety on until you are ready to shoot.
5. Be sure of your target before you pull the trigger; know the identifying features of the game you're after.
6. Never point a gun at anything you do not intend to shoot; avoid all horseplay while handling a gun.
7. Unattended guns should be unloaded; guns and ammunition should be stored separately beyond reach of children and careless adults.
8. Never climb a tree or fence or jump a ditch with a loaded gun; never pull a gun toward you by the muzzle.
9. Never shoot a bullet at a flat, hard surface or the surface of water; when at target practice, be sure your backstop is adequate.
10. Avoid alcoholic drinks before or during shooting.

The 10 Commandments of Safety are common sense rules that should govern the handling of all firearms.

HABITS OF SAFETY

The first one is, "Treat every gun with the respect due a loaded gun." The inference of course is that only a loaded gun is dangerous, which is true enough. Without a cartridge or shell in magazine or chamber, a gun is a piece of pipe with mechanical embellishments, but no more dangerous than that piece of pipe. If you watch an experienced shooter, you will find that a habit of years' standing takes over the instant he picks up a gun—whatever the type. He first opens the action to be certain that there is no cartridge in the chamber. His next move is to look into the action to detect any cartridge there or in the magazine. He then closes the action slowly, reopens it and *again* examines it. Only then will he put the firearm to his shoulder and, when he does so, he seldom rests his finger on the trigger. He can, of course, since he has carefully assured himself that the gun is devoid of ammunition. The point is that a careful shooter *always* follows this ritual, whether the gun he is handling has just been fired by a companion, has just come from a dealer's rack, or has been lifted from his own gun cabinet. A careful shooter assumes a gun is loaded until he sees for himself that it is not. This is a matter of pure habit, and it's a good one to develop.

The second rule states that it is a good idea to break a gun down (when the action type permits this) if it is carried in a car and, in any event, a gun should be cased, even if the case is only a cloth bag. At home or at camp, when a gun is in the rack or cabinet, the action should be open if it is exposed to tampering by other persons. Guns with detachable magazines, particularly automatic pistols, should have their magazines removed when being stored away. Loaded magazines should be kept in a drawer or other place of concealment. Guns should be unloaded out of doors before bringing them into the home or camp building. (In cold weather, it is a good idea to leave them outdoors in a protected place rather than bring them directly into a warm room. If carried immediately indoors, condensation usually gathers in the action and this may cause freeze-up of the action or, at the least, a slow-down of firing pin movement with resultant misfires.)

FIELD CARRIES

So far we have been dealing with empty guns. But how about the gun ready for use? Here the firearm presents its full potential for harm, and rule #4 of the Commandments spells out the warning, "Always carry your gun so that you can control the direction of the muzzle . . ." To amplify this: rifles can safely be carried on a sling, with muzzle pointing harmlessly up; in the crook of the right elbow with muzzle toward the ground; or in the "trail carry," grasped at its balance point in the right hand and carried, muzzle forward, tilted toward the ground.

There are three good field carries for the shotgun. The most useful is with the gun cradled over the crook of the left elbow with the left hand grasping the stock just behind the pistol grip. This allows the gun to be tossed to the right when a bird flushes suddenly, while the shooting hand slides up the stock, grasps the pistol grip and mounts the gun to the shoulder as the left hand slides forward to support the front end of the firearm. This is, of course, a carry when the gunner is working alone or with his hunting partner on his *right*.

When you are working with a man on the *left*, or in heavy cover and brush

Carrying a rifle on a sling or carrying strap over your shoulder is not only safe and comfortable, but leaves your hands free for climbing and using binoculars.

If your rifle doesn't have a carrying strap, or if you might have to get off a fast shot, this is a safe and easy way to carry your gun.

This is called the "trail carry," especially used if you are carrying a carbine, as short barreled rifles are called.

that interferes with a comfortable left arm carry, a good switch is to carry the gun over the right shoulder, muzzle up, with trigger guard also up and with the trigger finger resting on the bottom of the guard. The gun can be brought down quickly from this position and readied for a swing on a bird in a fraction of a second.

The final effective carry is a bit slower to get ready for action. The gun is cradled in the crook of your right arm, its balance point resting on your fore arm, the muzzle pointed toward the ground. This is comfortable with many models, not so good with some pumps and autoloaders since their loading port rests directly on your forearm and may dig into the flesh.

A combination of things can render a handgun safe. First of all, it should be carried in a hip or shoulder holster whenever possible. (And of course a holster for the hunter is not the fast draw type; a belt holster especially should

With a hunting partner on your right, this is a safe way to carry a shotgun. These pictures also show you how to mount your gun from this position.

With a fellow shooter on your left, or when in heavy brush, carrying a shotgun over your right shoulder is comfortable, safe, and allows you to mount the gun quickly.

Some shotguns can be carried very comfortably in the crook of the arm. These photos show how the gun is mounted, fluidly and quickly, for a shot.

Handgun holsters for hunting use should keep the gun firmly in place; there is no need for fast draw types here.

have a strap or flap across its top to make sure the gun stays in until the gunner wants to take it out.) With revolvers, placing an empty cartridge in the chamber under the hammer, and placing the hammer on the safety or half-cock notch with a single action, will guarantee safety. With an automatic pistol, the chamber should be left empty until the arm is about to be used, and the safety should be on.

MECHANICAL SAFETY DEVICES

Of course *every* gun that has a safety should be carried in the field with that safety *on*. At first, shooters of the shotgun may feel that carrying the gun on safe may slow down their chances for a quick flushing bird. And, at first, this may be true. But the demands of safety are far more important. Keep that gun on safe until the final instant when the gun is being mounted and readied to fire. You will find that it takes only a small amount of practice

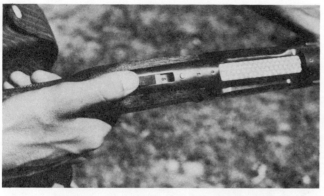 

If you are going to be handling a firearm, one of the first things you should know about it is the position of its safety. Seven common safeties are illustrated in these photographs. In the left row from top to bottom you see a standard tang safety, a cross bolt safety at the rear of the trigger guard, a "roll" safety, and a laterally moving tang safety. In the right row, again from top to bottom, there is a cross bolt safety at the front of the trigger guard, a thumb operated latch on the right side of the receiver, and a thumb operated latch on the left side of the receiver. Get the feel of the safety on any gun you're going to shoot, flicking it on and off until you are thoroughly familiar with its operation.

Here is how not *to bring the hammer back—either to full cock or half-cock—on a hammer gun. If you just use the ball of your thumb for this operation, the hammer may slip, especially if your hand is cold or sweaty, causing accidental discharge of the arm.*

The way to bring the hammer back is to wrap the first joint of the thumb around it. This offers a more secure hold, and there is therefore less danger of having the hammer slip.

to snap off the safety button as the gun comes up. In time you will do this without even thinking about it—and that's the way it should be.

Safety devices on rifles and shotguns are of many types: a sliding button on the upper tang, a push button either in the front or the rear of the trigger guard; in some rifles, notably bolt actions, the safety is a "roll" button near the rear of the receiver, or a thumb operated latch on the right or left side of the receiver, sometimes with a cocking indicator at the rear of the bolt. Train yourself to be so familiar with the location and operation of the safety that you can snap it off instinctively, with no conscious thought. It takes practice, to be sure, but it is the only safe way to carry a firearm.

Almost all shoulder arms with exposed hammers, some autoloading pistols of this type, and single action revolvers can be particularly dangerous since such guns have no safety device other than the half-cock position of the hammer. However, when the hammer is set in this position, the gun is safe enough. The problem is that there are times when a shooter's hands are either numb with cold or slippery with sweat and the hammer slips out from under the

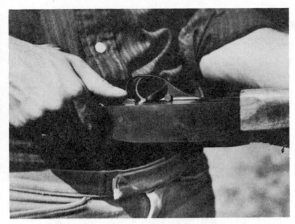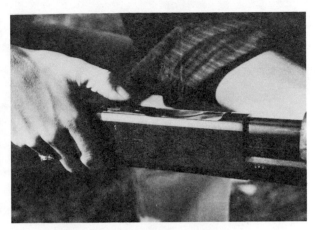

The action lock release on pump rifles, first photo, and shotguns, second photo, allows the action to be opened even though an unfired cartridge has just been chambered in the arm. Unless this release is pressed, the forearm of the gun stays locked in place.

thumb as it is being cocked or moved to the half-cock position. It is a good trick to cock all hammer guns with the first joint, rather than with the ball, of the thumb. The joint curves around the hammer and gives much more secure and sensitive contact. In putting the gun on half-cock, the hammer should be drawn back carefully, slowly, and *no farther* than is required to reach the half-cock position. Some shooters pull the hammer all the way to full-cock, and then, holding it with the thumb, pull the trigger to release it and "ride" the hammer down to the half-cock position. This is the most obvious situation in which the hammer can slip and fire the gun accidentally, especially if the tip of the thumb is used and it is numb or wet.

Shooters of modern firearms will have little trouble with safety devices. In every design, the safety successfully prevents the gun from firing. Safeties on bolt action rifles, in addition to blocking the movement of the trigger, also lock the bolt in the closed, or firing, position. Pump action rifles and shotguns also include an action lock. This prevents the opening of the action of a gun with a cartridge in the chamber until that cartridge is fired or until you depress the action lock release to open the breechblock. Automatic pistols usually incorporate more than one safety device in their design. In addition to a regular safety, some of these guns add a grip safety that allows the gun to be fired only when the hand depresses the grip latch as the trigger is squeezed in the act of firing. Other models lock the action against firing when the magazine is removed, so that the gun cannot be discharged if a cartridge is inadvertently left in the chamber. In other words, modern firearms have enough safety devices if we will but use them.

Many autoloading pistols have more than one safety device. The arrows in this picture point to the conventional thumb safety and the grip safety; the former must be flicked to its "off" position for the gun to fire and the latter is depressed by the shooting hand as you pull the trigger.

The normal safety measures used to protect the innocent bystander are obvious enough. No one aims a gun at anything he doesn't want to shoot. He makes certain before he shoots that he has a solid background that will catch a stray bullet without harm to people, animals, or property. A hunter of big game and varmints learns to distinguish a man from an animal, even if he can only see that man's head peeping over the horizon. Knowledge of the game hunted thus becomes a safety factor in protecting other hunters in the area.

The fact that a hunter wears bright clothing—red, yellow, or orange, usually —is no real guarantee of protection. Colors can blend into shadows, and the actual color value becomes obscured. The important point is to know just what the outline of the game animal should be. Only in rare instances will that outline resemble that of a man. The rule, naturally, is not to shoot until you know *precisely* what your target is.

The shooter's own safety always comes under consideration. The truth is that a large share of gunshot wounds are self-inflicted as a result of carelessness or ignorance. No one, for example, leans a loaded gun against a tree or fence when hunting dogs are frisking around. And it's not a good idea to do this even where no dogs are present. A gust of wind can push over a gun that's precariously balanced, and it is possible for a falling gun to discharge when it strikes the ground.

When crossing fences, guns should have actions open. When negotiating any tricky terrain—rock slides, ice patches, swamps, etc.—it is good insurance to unload the gun. It is unlikely that game will be spotted in time for a shot under these circumstances anyway, and if it does appear, it is only the work of a moment to slip a cartridge into the chamber or to operate the action to feed a fresh load into firing position. A hard fall when carrying a loaded gun can lead to an accidental discharge, sometimes with serious results.

BARREL OBSTRUCTIONS

For yet another reason, a fall with a gun can be trouble. If the gun strikes muzzle first—as it often does—you may find the bore plugged with mud, clay, snow, or other debris. Shooting such a plugged bore will usually result in some sort of damage to the gun and, rather often, damage to the shooter. A plugged barrel can burst completely or split, releasing bits of the cartridge brass which will often inflict eye damage. Always check your gun bore after a hard fall even though you may not believe the muzzle struck the ground.

Other types of gun bore obstructions can also be dangerous. Occasionally, a shooter will carelessly leave a piece of cleaning patch in the bore of a gun or, with shotguns, it can happen that a faulty load will leave wads in the bore. Shooting another shell through such a bore will usually split the barrel if the wads happen to be in the right spot to build up maximum pressure. If, then, when you fire a shotgun and detect less than the usual report or recoil, examine the bore before you attempt to fire another shell through it.

High power rifles have also been blown up with serious injury to the shooter who fires an improper load; i.e., a cartridge for which the rifle is not chambered. For example, shooters have been known to fire 8mm cartridges in rifles chambered for .30/06. This develops extremely high pressures, since the 8mm bullet is much larger than the .30 caliber bore. If the rifle does not have a

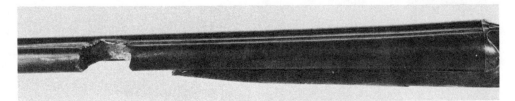

Splitting, or bursting, can result if a barrel is plugged by any debris. Frequently this results in injury to the shooter.

particularly strong receiver, it will usually blow up in the shooter's face with tragic results. It is always poor practice, if the rifle's caliber is not definitely known, to "try" several cartridges in the chamber. The fact that a cartridge will enter the chamber and the action can be closed is no proof that the cartridge fits that rifle. This is a common mistake with owners of military surplus rifles that are unmarked as to caliber, and it is a bad one.

Obstructions in barrels will not necessarily blow up a gun, since the result depends upon what type of obstruction is involved and just where it lies within the bore. However, such obstructions can build pressures to the point where they may rupture the cartridge case, which in turn can spray hot gasses and bits of brass into a shooter's eyes. Large lensed shatterproof shooting glasses are always good insurance against such accidents, and many shooters wear these every time they fire a gun.

Accidents with firearms differ widely in their cause and effect. Yet very few, if any, are traceable to faulty arms or factory ammunition. Rather, the shooter is careless or is ignorant of what he should do with his gun. Many accidental discharges have occurred because a shooter checked the reliability of his safety by pulling the trigger of a loaded gun. If a safety is to be checked in this way, the gun should, obviously, be unloaded. Another common accident is caused by a shooter inadvertently dropping a 20 gauge shell into a 12 gauge gun (where it passes through the chamber out of sight and lodges in the bore), then inserting and firing a 12 gauge load in the gun. Understandably, with most guns this creates mayhem, usually injuring the shooter.

Many shooters wear shatterproof glasses every time they fire a gun; the chance of injury from hot gasses or bits of brass from a ruptured cartridge are greatly lessened when such glasses are worn.

And now, in these days of great interest in reloading ammunition, it is vital that the novice hand loader heed the instruction manuals in his choice of powder types and amounts of charge. Accidents have happened when the reloader has charged rifle cartridges with powder meant for use in either shotgun or pistol cartridges. The only necessary precaution is to *read* the data in reloading manuals and then keep your wits about you when carrying out the various steps. Reloading ammo is *not* dangerous; only when it is done by a careless person who is ignorant of the requirements and is too lazy to study them can danger result.

It would be quite easy to fill a book with specific, detailed causes of accidents with firearms. These are legion in both cause and result. Yet it is a rare case indeed when the cause cannot be traced to negligence, carelessness, or ignorance on the part of the shooter. It must again be said that guns in themselves are not dangerous—the danger lies only with the people using them.

Chapter 2

HOW TO SHOOT
SMALL BORE RIFLES

Perhaps the most familiar gun in America today is the .22 rifle. Ammunition for it is inexpensive, its recoil is practically nonexistent, and its report not at all bothersome. It is the "fun gun" of the shooting world, consumer of more ammunition than any other caliber. Although it was originally designed for hunting small game, it has no peer as the basic arm for teaching.

Four distinct types of .22 rifles are made in the United States: bolt action, pump action, lever action, and semiautomatic. While we have chosen a single shot bolt action for our teaching arm, the shooter should understand how each type functions.

UNDERSTANDING THE ACTIONS

A bolt action firearm operates by activating a steel encased firing pin mechanism located in a grooved channel inside the bolt. The hand propelled mechanism, the bolt, loads a cartridge at the completion of each cycle; manual operation makes this the safest and most dependable type of rifle action. In a few single shot models, the firing pin is cocked by the shooter pulling back on a knurled knob at the end of the bolt. This compresses the firing pin spring and locks it into place as the sear (notched trigger tail) settles into the base of the pin itself. Pressure on the trigger unseats the sear and frees the firing pin, which is propelled by its spring against the primer of the shell, causing it to discharge.

In a pump (or slide) action rifle, the bolt assembly is activated by the extension of an arm that runs from the sliding fore end, or pump, of the rifle into the action housing and works directly against the bolt. When the shooter pulls back the fore end with his left hand, the action slides back inside the housing, cocking and feeding the rifle with its back-and-forth cycles.

Lever actions, like the bolt and slide actions, are hand operated. The bolt assembly in these models, activated by a finger lever pivoting on a screw, carries the bolt to the rear, ejecting the empty case and cocking the gun as the lever is forced down by the shooting hand. Closing the lever to its original position returns the bolt, picks up a fresh cartridge from the magazine, and chambers it as the bolt locks into final position.

The principle of the semiautomatic (or autoloading) action is based on two separate and distinct operations. For the first shot, the bolt assembly must be hand activated to cock the arm, but on subsequent shots the gun cocks and feeds itself without further attention from the shooter. When a shot is fired, gas is formed by the burning powder within the chamber, and its force is utilized to thrust back the bolt, eject the spent shell, cock the hammer, and pick up another cartridge from the feed slide as the bolt is slammed back into place by a heavy action-spring. In a semiautomatic action, the arm must be trigger-fired each time; in a fully automatic action (used primarily by the military), the shells are fired by each forward movement of the bolt during the firing cycle, which lasts as long as the shooter keeps his finger on the trigger and cartridges remain in the magazine.

In a .22 caliber arm, the cartridge is fired by what we call the rim-fire method. Rather than striking a center primer and discharging the shell, the firing pin is set so that it hits the outer edge of the case-rim head, much as a cap is exploded in a toy pistol. This blow ignites a priming mixture within the rim of the cartridge, which in turn ignites the powder charge in the shell and starts the bullet.

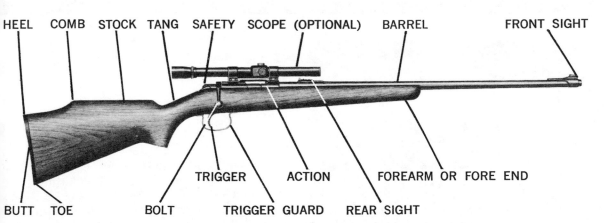

Here is a typical .22 bolt action rifle, its parts labeled for easy identification. These parts are the same for bigger caliber bolt actions, and with the exception of the operating parts that take the place of the bolt on other shoulder arms, this gun can serve as a model for all long arms. Familiarize yourself with these parts before you fire a gun.

1

3

5

These sequence photographs show the steps in the operation of a bolt action arm: lifting the bolt and pulling it all the way to the rear gets rid of the empty shell that was in the chamber; pushing the bolt forward and turning it down chambers a fresh cartridge and locks the action. The movement of the bolt also cocks the rifle.

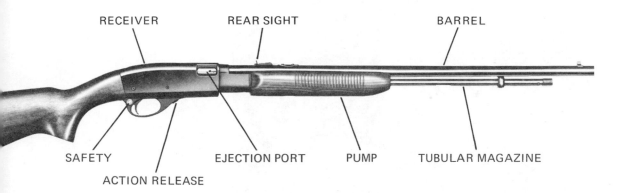

RECEIVER   REAR SIGHT   BARREL

SAFETY   EJECTION PORT   PUMP   TUBULAR MAGAZINE

ACTION RELEASE

This labeled photo of a pump action shows the parts that you should be able to identify before you use such a gun.

A back-and-forth movement operates a pump action. Pulling the fore end back extracts and ejects the empty shell and cocks the gun; pushing the fore end into its forward position chambers a loaded shell and locks the action.

A *downward and upward movement of the lever operates a lever action rifle. The downward movement throws the used shell out of the gun and cocks it for the next shot; returning the lever to its closed position chambers a fresh shell and locks the action.*

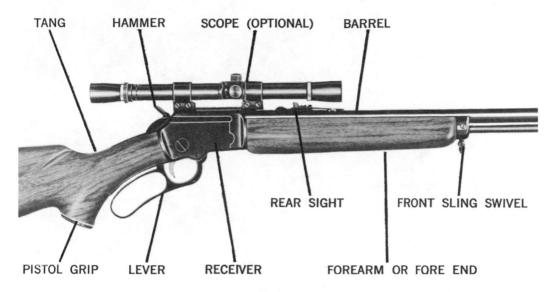

TANG   HAMMER   SCOPE (OPTIONAL)   BARREL

REAR SIGHT   FRONT SLING SWIVEL

PISTOL GRIP   LEVER   RECEIVER   FOREARM OR FORE END

This is typical lever action rifle.

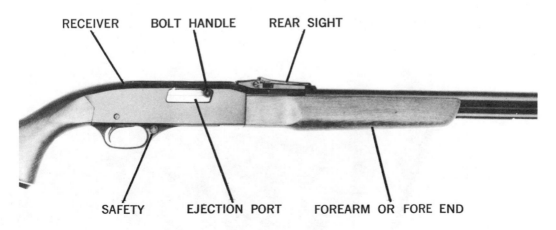

RECEIVER   BOLT HANDLE   REAR SIGHT

SAFETY   EJECTION PORT   FOREARM OR FORE END

Here is typical autoloading action.

For the first shot with an auto-loading arm, the bolt mechanism must be worked manually. To do this, you simply pull back the bolt handle and let it snap forward, or press an action release button. This moves a cartridge into the chamber and cocks and locks the gun.

After manually cocking the gun, as in the preceding picture, each shot can be fired by simply pressing the trigger. The gun automatically ejects the fired shell and is cocked—as the bolt assembly moves rearward—and chambers a fresh shell and locks itself—as the bolt rams forward.

THE FIRST STEP

For the first lesson, we chose a single shot, bolt action, automatic cocking Colt Colteer .22 rifle. This arm has the simplicity of a single shot while incorporating the safety features of larger rifles. When in position, its manually operated safety makes it almost impossible to discharge the arm. We say "almost" because a mechanical difficulty or a worn part can give the lie to the strongest statement.

Regardless of the small size of the bullet and the relatively light powder charge propelling it, the .22 is lethal, dangerous within a mile. For this reason, it should be handled with respect, not only for the shooter's own sake but for that of his associates as well. A gun can kill; even the supposedly harmless air rifle can be fatal if its pellet hits certain parts of the body.

The best way to become accustomed to the way a firearm functions is by handling it. Remove the bolt—by holding back the trigger and slipping the bolt out to the rear—and examine the gun; identify and learn the various parts, using the labeled photograph on page 17 as a reference. Then put the bolt back—by holding the trigger in its rearward position and sliding the bolt forward into the receiver. Now shoulder the gun a few times, gradually becoming accustomed to its weight and feel.

THE SIGHT PICTURE

The key to precise rifle shooting is the sight picture. Its importance cannot be too strongly stressed. Err by one-sixteenth of an inch when you line up the front and rear sights and the bull's-eye, and your bullet will be feet wide of the target at 100 paces.

Lining up a set of iron sights, you will see three objects simultaneously: the rear sight, the front sight, and the target. To hit the bull's-eye, each element must be aligned in what shooters call the "sight picture."

The rear sight is notched; the Colteer's notch is in the shape of a half-moon. (Others are shaped like V's or squared-off U's.) The front sight on the Colteer is a square topped blade, presenting a blocklike appearance from the rear. Other front sights are topped with a small bead. For perfect alignment with standard open, or iron, sights, the front sight should be seen as sitting squarely in the middle of the rear sight notch, the top of the blade or bead being level with the top of the sides of the notch. Gently perched atop this two element grouping is the target. This is the correct sight picture, and it is universally called the six o'clock hold.

There are two things, then, that must align precisely with the rear sight: the front sight, which is to be centered from left to right in—and even with

Here is the perfect sight picture: the front sight is centered perfectly in the rear sight notch and the target is perched on top of the front sight. Note that there are three elements to align with this sighting set-up.

the top of—the rear sight notch, and the bull's-eye, which seems to sit gently on the front sight blade. You'll miss the bull if the front sight is too far to one side, too high or too low in the rear sight notch, or if the target is too high, too low or to either side in this picture.

Another sight combination is one that employs a peep instead of the open rear. This device is nothing but a small hole drilled into a metal block. Look through it and your eye automatically will center the front sight in the peep's hole. Now it is just a matter of visually placing the bull's-eye on top of the front sight blade.

In all shooting with iron sights, a beginning shooter, for no particular reason, will automatically close his left eye in aligning the sights. Long experience has proved that the best marksmen using rifle, handgun, or shotgun, keep both eyes open for a clearer view of the target, since man is a two eyed animal and his depth of vision is only effective when both eyes are open. It's only a matter of brief practice before your right eye will unconsciously align the sights and your left eye will watch the target.

It's rare for a right-handed shooter to be hindered by a left master eye. (By master eye we mean the eye which directs a person's vision.) Anyone can check to determine which of his eyes is the master by a simple test: with both eyes open, you point a finger at a small object; you then close the left eye and if the right eye and the finger are aligned on the object, you are a

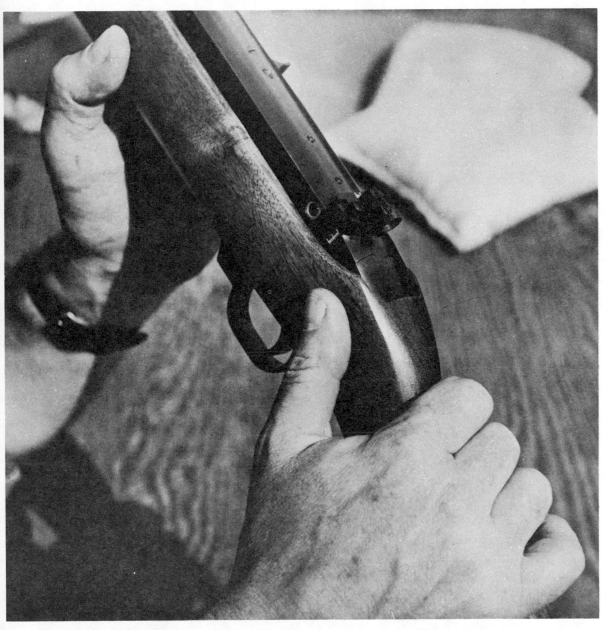

Here is a typical receiver, or peep, sight. To get a sight picture with this device, you just have to look through it and get the front sight in its proper position in relation to the target. Only two elements must be aligned here, the front sight with the target; your eye should automatically center the front sight in the peep's aperture.

Despite the universal tendency of beginning shooters to close one eye when firing a gun, both eyes should be kept open at all times. One eye acts as the "master" in aiming, while the other increases depth perception and peripheral vision.

The right eye is the master eye for most right-handers. A simple test will determine which one is your master eye.

No alignment of various elements of a sight is necessary if you use a scope. Just place the crosshairs on the target, and if the rifle is properly sighted-in, your bullet will hit where the crosshairs meet.

right-eyed person. If, of course, when you close the left eye, you find your finger pointing to the left of the object, your left eye is your master eye. You can confirm this by closing your right eye and you will find that the left eye lines up with your finger and the object.

If you find that your left eye is the master eye, you'll have to do one of two things. Either learn to shoot from the left shoulder or deliberately, though it is less desirable, close the left eye; this sometimes allows the right to become the master eye. Some shooters buy special glasses and cover the left lens to blank out the vision, which relieves the left eye of continuous strain if much shooting is to be done.

The use of a telescopic sight totally eliminates the need for coordination between front and rear sights. A look through the scope shows a pair of crosshairs (or other type alignment device). Where these crosshairs meet is where the bullet will hit if the rifle is sighted-in properly. All the shooter has to do with a scope is center the crosshairs on the heart of the bull's-eye and squeeze the trigger.

THE "MAGIC V"

The thumb and forefinger, working together, form the "Magic V." By an almost offsetting action, these two digits control each other in a perfect sequence. The forefinger, or trigger finger, presses toward the shooter's shoulder, while the thumb offsets the trigger movement. Incorrect thumb position and pressure will frequently result in faulty shot groups. The remaining fingers control stock position.

The thumb should follow the line of the tang, resting lightly at first, then with controlled pressure. Properly set, the thumb rides the tang just to the right of the vertical, sliding almost automatically into position as proficiency increases. With the three remaining fingers clasping the pistol grip, the thumb controls the pressure of the hand on the stock.

The forefinger exerts the smallest amount of pressure of any of the five fingers at the instant of firing. The tip, or pad, of the first joint presses the trigger, taking up the slack in the mechanism so gradually that the actual firing almost comes as a surprise to the shooter.

This photo shows the proper position of the shooting hand on a rifle. Note especially the placement of the thumb; it does not cross the tang, but is placed parallel to it.

THE IMPORTANCE OF BREATH CONTROL

Man's physiology prevents him from holding a firearm absolutely steady, for his heartbeat—despite the best efforts of will and muscle—causes a minute barrel waver. As a result, breath control, plus conditioning one's body to minimize the motion of the gun, is perhaps the hardest lesson to learn.

Shooting requires the close coordination of brain, hands, and eyes. The hands do the muscular work, the eyes direct, and the brain reacts on signal. But how can the unsteadiness caused by breathing and heartbeat be controlled? The answer is to take advantage of the process of exhalation, the time when the body is steadiest. As the chest cavity depresses to exhale breath from the lungs, the muscles, satisfied by the intake of oxygen, rest for a split second. The correct trigger squeeze, at the instant when exhalation is about half completed and is momentarily halted, results in good let-off of your shot.

Dry firing—or discharging an arm without live ammunition in the chamber —points up many early faults. (To protect the firing pin during dry firing, it is a good idea to have a fired cartridge case in the chamber.) The element of surprise—the shooter not actually knowing when the firing pin will be released to fire the cartridge—is all-important. The trigger should be treated gently and delicately, not manhandled.

The firing of a rifle is made up of several steps:

1. As the index finger, its tip touching the trigger, begins to pick up the trigger slack, the shooter should be "at the top of a breath," or just at the point of exhaling.

2. When the gentle exhalation begins, the pressure on the trigger increases.

3. As it increases, the thumb counteracts it by exerting opposing pressure.

4. While the thumb is compensating for the pressure on the trigger, the other three fingers around the pistol grip offset the thumb's pressure by their own vertical pressure. In short, the rearward, lateral, and horizontal pressures in the firing cycle are counteracted by different parts of the hand.

5. Perfect release occurs when the breath is half to three-quarters expelled, then held for an instant as the shot is squeezed off. The actual ignition of the cartridge should come almost as a surprise, at the end of a gradual process, for conscious pulling of the trigger causes a flinch or yank that sends the shot off target.

Once the preceding steps are mastered, any shooter who learns the firing positions can become a good shot through practice. Now let's deal with each position in detail.

The four basic positions in firing a rifle are: bench, prone, sitting, and offhand. Let's discuss them in the order in which they should be learned.

BENCH

When sitting at a shooting bench, the gunner enjoys the benefits of sand-bags and barrel support in addition to a stable, unwavering shooting platform that helps him gain confidence and skill.

The fore end of the rifle is rested on a sandbagged prop. The toe of the stock is also placed on a sandbag for stability. This insures that the rifle will hold steady on target, affording the best possible sight picture.

The shooter now aligns the sights on the target, adjusting the sandbags so that the movement of the rifle will be slight, even when he lets go of it.

Moving a piano stool or other seating device toward the rear of the bench, he assumes a position with his left hand grasping the forearm of the rifle behind the sandbags and the right on the stock and trigger; both elbows rest on the bench. He places his cheek firmly and well forward on the comb and checks his right hand for the "Magic V" position.

A shooting bench, since it is a great aid to steadiness, is the place for a beginning shooter to start.

PRONE

The shooter lies flat on his stomach, his body 45 degrees off the line of sight, his legs extended. The left and right elbows form a tripod with the body to make a shooting platform. The left elbow rests directly under the fore end of the rifle, creating an up-and-down brace that is called a "forehand cradle." The feet rest on their sides with the toes pointing out. Extending the right elbow to a 45 degree angle with the shoulders keeps both shoulders level in relation to the ground, resulting in greater stability and shooting comfort.

Next is the prone position; with left elbow firmly set and the shooter's body comfortably and steadily stretched out, this is the steadiest natural position without a support.

The sitting position, because the arms are supported and the body is relaxed, is also a steady position.

SITTING

The shooter sits with feet and legs extending 45 degrees from the line of sight, elbows on knees to insure a solid shooting platform; the heels are dug in slightly to afford control. Bow the back and shoulders, thus forming a pocket in the shoulder into which the butt of the rifle is cushioned.

OFFHAND

The body address is about 90 degrees off target, with the feet parallel and about 12 inches apart. The left arm is tucked down and under the fore end with the hand forming a cradle in which the fore end rests; the right elbow is at a 90-degree angle to the body and parallel to the ground. The position of the thumb and hand remains the same as in the other stances.

The hardest position to master is off-hand; there is no rest for the arms and no support for the body.

ON-TARGET ANALYSIS OF FAULTS

An experienced gunner can glance at a group of shots punched into a target (assuming the rifle used was sighted-in, and then fired from this sighted-in range) and tell a beginner what is wrong with his trigger release. Straying shots are the result of mistakes; pinpointing faults early prevents them from becoming serious later on. Looking at a target as if it were the face of a clock, let's analyze some common errors.

Shots in the 12–3 o'clock quadrant: This is the result of incorrect thumb pressure. As the shooter increased trigger pull, he forgot to compensate with his thumb, thus allowing the shots to climb high and to the right.

Shots in the 3–6 o'clock quadrant: Too strong thumb pressure combined with too tight a hold on the pistol grip by the other three fingers pulled the barrel (and the shots) down and to the right.

Shots in the 6–9 o'clock quadrant: This is caused by excessive pistol grip pressure and not enough thumb pressure at the instant of trigger let-off.

Shots in the 9–12 o'clock quadrant: Insufficient thumb pressure plus too strong left pressure of the fingers on the pistol grip permitted the barrel to climb, and forced the shots high and to the left.

It is apparent that a beginning shooter can make different hold and trigger squeeze errors from shot to shot. This will spread his hits over various parts of the target, in all quadrants, which will be confounding for a time—until he learns to "call the shot." And until this milestone is reached, he will have some difficulties in knowing just what he is doing wrong.

In simplest terms, calling the shot is nothing more than remembering just where the sights rested in relation to the target when the rifle fired. The experienced rifleman retains this picture clearly after recoil of the gun blots out his view. Then, when he checks his target, it is usually only a matter of confirming what his eye predicted would be there. If a skilled shooter fires wide of the mark—provided his rifle is correctly sighted—he will know it before the bullet reaches the target. No shooter can call himself a rifleman until this skill of calling the shot becomes firmly established in coordination between eye and brain. A "flincher"—who is necessarily a trigger-jerker rather than a squeezer—never conditions himself to develop this vital skill in rifle shooting.

REPETITION AND CORRECTION

As with all sports, practice makes the difference. To become a shooter of even modest ability, one must fire plenty of ammunition. Once the gunner has learned positions, plus holding and firing techniques, he is ready for actual shooting. Working from each of the four positions, he should fire away, paying far more attention to form than to accuracy at the outset. As his familiarity with a position becomes a habit, he can start checking the location of his shots on the target. Then he should make it a weekly (if not daily) practice to "shoot for record" from each of the four positions, after which he should take each target and analyze every shot, understanding why a particular shot hit where it did and what mistakes were made.

Repetition may be dull, but it is the best way to develop into a shooter. While a few of us possess the excellent coordination of hand and eye that one finds in a "natural," the majority need step-by-step instruction so that their bad habits can be corrected before they become set.

Chapter 3

HOW TO SHOOT BIG BORE
AND VARMINT RIFLES

Every sport has its hurdles. In flying it's that "alone" feeling when you've taken off on your first solo flight, leaving your instructor on the field to sweat you back to a safe landing. In diving it may be your first effort from the three meter board. In shooting a rifle it faces you the day you become proficient with rim-fire arms and are ready to shoot a center-fire cartridge. For with the simple impact of firing pin on primer, you experience two sensations that must be coped with and mastered—recoil and report.

Like .22 rifles, center-fires comprise four basic types—bolt, pump, lever, and semiautomatic—but where the .22 is a teaching arm that may be used for plinking, target shooting, and small game hunting, the heavy caliber center-fire is a powerhouse that packs a terrific wallop. For this reason it is wise to familiarize yourself with its workings and become accustomed to its feel before shooting it.

WHAT IS CALIBER?

In the infancy of gunsmithing, when there was no standardization of approach, caliber depended pretty much on whim. A gunsmith in Pennsylvania might make a rifle with a bore that measured .3897 of an inch and then mold a ball to fit it, but the purchaser of the gun would find it impossible to duplicate the bullet mold in, say, Kansas without having it especially made.

Misconceptions about caliber are rampant. For example, how is one to know that a .303 Savage really measures .300 of an inch; that a .32/20 Winchester is .3045 of an inch; that the old .32 rim-fire Marlin was .302 caliber and a .38/55 was .370 caliber? Then there was the Martini-Henry rifle of 1871. Its designation was .577/450. Was it .45 caliber or .58 caliber? (The answer is that it was .45 caliber.)

While readings are standardized today, here are two simple definitions that will be useful: the caliber of the rifle is the diameter of the bore; bullet diameter is always a bit larger than bore diameter so that the rifling can effectively grip and stabilize the bullet before it begins its flight. For example, the .308 Winchester cartridge is fired in a .30 caliber bore.

RIFLING

When gunsmiths discovered that the flight of a spinning projectile was steadier and more accurate than one that didn't spin, the intricate process we know as "rifling" was born. Rifling is the cutting of a series of grooves, resembling those of a slow-pitch thread, in a rifle or handgun bore. Just as a screw seats itself by turning on its threads as it is forced by a screwdriver, a bullet propelled through a rifle barrel follows the lands and grooves of the rifling. Think of the lands as the shoulders of the thread which the screw follows and the grooves as the base of the threading. The lands grasp the projectile as it traverses the grooves in its progress toward the muzzle, and they impart the spin as it takes off in flight.

LOADING AND UNLOADING

Before you find out how to put cartridges into and remove them from large caliber rifles, you should learn a little about these loads. Pick one up; feel its weight and size and you'll begin to understand the power it can gen-

Here is an unfired cartridge and, next to it, the bullet from that cartridge after it has hit its target and expanded.

erate and the force of its impact. Look at the photo accompanying this passage; it shows, next to a loaded cartridge, the expansion of the bullet *after* it hits a target. It's a short jump to understanding the damage a high power bullet is capable of and the respect it deserves.

Now let's start with the guns. Many bolt operated large caliber rifles have an action-contained magazine—a depressed-spring carrier seated in the base of the magazine housing, which acts as a shell reservoir. To load, you must open the action and insert the shells into the magazine; to unload, you must work the bolt—each cartridge must be carried into the chamber and then extracted and ejected. A feature built into some bolt actions is a quick release floor plate at the bottom of the magazine. This permits fast unload-

This view into an action-contained magazine shows the cartridges as they are held in the rifle.

A quick release floor plate allows cartridges to be taken from the rifle without working each one through the action.

A detachable box magazine, loaded with cartridges, is about to be inserted into a big bore rifle.

This photograph shows cartridge placement in a double column magazine.

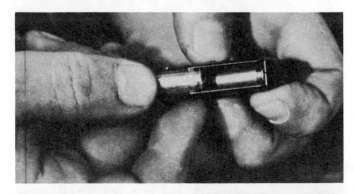

Here is a single column magazine, used in center-fire rifles chambered for short cartridges and in .22s.

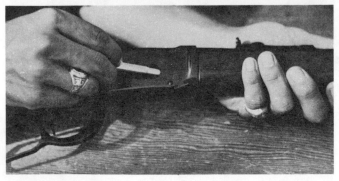

In a typical "side loader," cartridges are fed into the magazine past a tongue that depresses to permit their entry.

ing without working each cartridge through the action. This is a convenience, but cartridges must still be loaded one at a time.

The easiest loading and unloading method involves a detachable box magazine employed in some big bore rifles. For these arms, the part holding the ammunition is detachable from the arm itself. You can therefore completely empty the rifle except for a chambered cartridge in one motion, and slam a full magazine back into place to load it.

Among the best known of currently made American high power rifles—in addition to the Remington Model 760, which is a rather unusual pump action—the Browning BLR (lever), Mossberg 810 (bolt), and Remington 742 (auto) and 788 (bolt) all have detachable magazines. The Savage 99 (lever) and 110 (bolt) are available with either integral or detachable magazines. These use a double column system, meaning that the cartridges are staggered in two rows, side by side, just as they are in the integral magazines of so many bolt action rifles. Some older rifles and imports, employing short actions for short cartridges like the .22 Hornet, have detachable magazines loaded in a single column, as in .22 rim-fire rifles.

Big caliber lever and pump action guns have one basic feature that should be emphasized. Like all rifles with tubular magazines (and most big bore levers and pumps store their ammunition this way), they are sometimes loaded when you think they are empty. A shell may "hang up" inside the tube and not be noticed in a cursory check. These guns should be opened and closed several times, to see whether a loaded cartridge shows on the carrier.

All heavy caliber lever and pump actions with tubular magazines are "side loaders." Whereas in .22s the cartridges are fed into the tube from the forward end, in big guns they are fed into the side of the receiver past a tongue that depresses to permit their entry. This tongue is set in the side of the action plate and as each shell passes it, the spring in the magazine becomes more and more depressed until capacity is reached. The expansion of this spring propels the rearmost cartridge from the tube into the action, where it is picked up by the carrier and seated by the bolt for firing.

Be sure to acquaint yourself thoroughly with the loading and unloading process of each rifle you are going to shoot. Become so familiar with the operation that you can do it with your eyes closed.

THE FIRST FIRING

It is a law of physics that for every action there is an opposite reaction—a truth that is demonstrated every time you fire a high power rifle. The action of firing causes two things to take place instantaneously: an unusual amount of noise, and recoil. The best way to overcome any fear that may build up in your mind before the actual firing is to know what to expect.

Recoil does not affect everyone in the same way. Some football players, for example, enjoy body contact and shock; without them we would not have linemen. All of us who engage in sports have been hit without minding it particularly, and the recoil from the average rifle is no greater than a healthy shove or swat. In big bores such as the Weatherby .460 Magnum, the Winchester .458 African, and the Holland & Holland .600 double, however, the recoil is severe. Designed to stop huge, heavy boned animals in their tracks, these arms generate more than two tons of muzzle energy—enough to flatten a charging elephant. But they are intended for the biggest of big game hunting and need not concern us here.

One new development of the past decade has had some effect on current concepts of recoil. This was Remington's Model 1100 shotgun, a gas operated autoloader incorporating a newly designed piston which causes the gas formed by the shell's burning powder to spread over a wider area than previously, while special inertia weights let the gun itself momentarily absorb some of the kick. Although this kick is retransmitted from the gun to the shoulder, the total recoil has been slowed down (without slowing down the functioning of the gun) and the shooter therefore *feels* less of a belt. The Model 1100 cuts the recoil effect in 12 gauge by about 50 percent. This principle may someday be applied to rifles.

Other manufacturers have occasionally experimented with variations on the same theme. There are also recoil-reducing devices designed for insertion into the stock of a gun. Some of these work on principles involving weight and inertia. They do cut recoil effect somewhat but, of course, they also alter a gun's weight and balance. Another approach in recent years was a hydraulic shock absorber that could be installed inside a stock.

Some of these inventions have been welcomed by trap and skeet shooters, who may put hundreds of shells through a gun in one day, and must therefore stand up to a heavy battering if they use a 12 gauge gun. Veteran hunters, whether they use rifles or shotguns, usually don't care enough about recoilless shooting to spend money for a recoil-reducing unit. They say that during any single day in the field they simply don't get so many shots that the punishment of recoil is more than they can take. And since most gun models won't feature recoil reduction for a long time to come, anyone learning to shoot a big bore firearm must still learn to handle heavy recoil.

Just as you would not give a youngster his first driving lesson with a 10 ton truck, you should not expect him to make the jump from a .22 to a .30/06 in a single step. Since the best results are obtained by approaching the large calibers gradually, the following pattern may be helpful. These are the arms—and the order in which they were used—to graduate a typical beginning .22 shooter into a gunner competent with big bore rifles.

ADJUSTMENT BY CALIBER PROGRESSION

1. .22 Magnum. With this gun, still in the rim-fire class but with considerably more velocity and power than conventional .22s, there is a slight recoil. Noise increase is proportionate to the increase in shell powder charge.

2. .222. Recoil gains in intensity but is still light. Noise sharp and fairly loud.

3. .243. Recoil is heavier and noise increases along with power, but by now the shooter is relaxed and isn't disturbed by either.

4. .25/06. In this, his first experience with a medium game cartridge, the gunner is now able to ride out the noise and recoil in good style.

5. .308. For the first time the shooter feels recoil in direct proportion to noise. By now, however, he is prepared for it. Not visible reaction, eager to continue.

6. .264 Magnum. A .264 is a .458 casing necked down to handle a 140 grain bullet, so recoil is fairly heavy from a shooting bench and noise tremendous. Gunner in fine shape.

At the completion of the series the shooter was still hale, hearty, and thoroughly enjoyed himself. Graduating by degrees over a period of several weeks, he found himself able to take the biggest calibers in stride. The whole business of careful trigger let-off regardless of caliber is a matter of will power—steeling the nerves and muscles for the shock of recoil against cheek and shoulder and the impact of a blast on the eardrums. Nothing but continuous shooting, preferably with low power rifles, will develop it. If you find, after some shooting with the big rifles, that you are beginning to flinch, *stop* right then and go back to the rim-fires for a refresher course.

HOW TO HANDLE RECOIL

Bench shooting, because the solid confines of the rest don't absorb any of the kick, subjects the gunner to maximum recoil. Therefore, once you have learned to handle the big bores from a rest you will be able to master the prone, sitting, and offhand positions easily.

In the lighter, varminting, calibers (.22 Magnum, .222, and .243 in our progression) recoil is slight. Considering the fact that a heavy 12 gauge shotgun shell generates more than 25 pounds of free recoil at the shoulder on firing (much more kick than 90 percent of the center-fire rifles produce), recoil can practically be discounted here. For that reason you are able to keep your left hand well out on the fore end when shooting these light, flat trajectory arms, thus increasing your holding efficiency without unconsciously bracing yourself for a shock.

Minor adjustments to recoil must be made in the bigger calibers. In our progression, we used a .25/06, a .308, and a .264 Magnum—each of which packs an increasing degree of medium to heavy recoil and has a loud muzzle blast. Handling any of these from a rest necessitates adjusting your hold. To form a big bore "cradle" (for these or any big caliber rifles), let the forearm of the gun rest on its own weight on the sandbagged forked rest. Put the butt plate solidly in the pocket formed by your right biceps and pectoral muscles, resting your right elbow on the bench and bringing your left hand over to clasp the biceps of your right arm. The butt is held in the shoulder pocket by the pressure exerted from below by your left thumb; this assures that the rifle is in position to distribute recoil over a wide area of your shoulder. The last three fingers of your right hand apply longitudinal pressure to the pistol grip of the stock.

In shooting from this cradle, don't forget to relax your stomach muscles as you exhale; this will prevent your being rigid at firing impact and you'll experience only slight discomfort from the recoil. One precaution: always wear earplugs, either the standard rubber ones, pads of cotton, or the ear protectors made especially for shooters, during *all* big bore target practice. (They are not practical while hunting, where there is no real risk of injury to your ears because you don't have a chance to take many shots in a short time.) Muzzle blast is injurious to the sensitive makeup of the ear and can be unpleasant—if not dangerous—without these aids. Big guns are loud guns and allowances should be made for them at all times.

The biceps and the edge of the pectoral muscles also form a natural pocket when a gun is fired without the benefit of a rest, and the butt plate should be snugged into this pocket before you fire. Settle the top of the butt plate

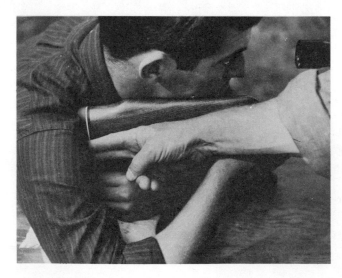

When shooting any hard recoiling rifle from a bench rest, make sure the butt plate is solidly in the pocket formed by your right biceps and pectoral muscles.

Your right elbow is on the bench; your left hand holds the biceps of your right arm, with the butt held in the shoulder pocket by the pressure of your left thumb.

Ear protectors, designed especially for shooters, should be worn when you're going to fire a big bore rifle repeatedly.

The biceps and pectoral muscles also form a pocket when you fire a big caliber shoulder arm without a rest. The butt is kept in this pocket by strong rearward pressure from the left hand.

just below the line of your collarbone, wedging it firmly into that protective nest of muscle tissue. To keep the stock tight against your shoulder, increase the rearward pressure on the gun by wrapping your left hand around the fore-arm—not in a "clutch for dear life," but simply to afford a stronger grip than was necessary when firing a .22.

When you are in the correct position, exhale about half of your breath and deliberately relax your stomach muscles. By doing this, you allow your body to "roll with the punch," acting much as springs and shock absorbers do when a car hits a bump. Absorbing recoil in this way lessens the sting without impairing the accuracy of your aim.

Remember in big bore firing never to tighten a muscle that is not involved in the act of shooting. The more relaxed you are, the better you shoot. In any case, overcoming the effect of recoil is largely a matter of will power, of steeling yourself to take it without tightening up and jerking at the trigger.

SHOOTING WHERE YOU LOOK

A bullet does not travel in a straight line. Regardless of the speed at which it starts, the force of gravity takes effect as soon as it leaves the muzzle. For this reason all bullets travel a course that leads to their coming down to the ground; this path is called a trajectory. Sight adjustment compensates for the bullet's drop.

Center-fire rifle projectiles travel at unbelievable speeds; some of the hot-shot varminters can send a bullet half a mile in a second—one tick of the clock and the slug is at the target! But regardless of their speed, bullets fall. Regardless of their weight, they are affected by wind. Therefore, sight adjustment is a delicate and important part of shooting. Since no rifle is worth its salt if it does not hit the target, let's discuss two methods that help insure this result:

1. Moving the rear sight determines where on the target the bullet will strike. Say the slug is hitting level with the center of the bull's-eye, but three inches to the right; moving the rear sight to the left will bring the bullet to the left. If the bullet hole is to the left, moving the sight to the right will move the point of impact in that direction. If the mark is high on the target, lowering the sight will drop the hit; if it is low on the target, raising the sight will raise the hit.

Many peep sights are the micrometer type—controlled by screws, minutely adjustable for windage (the right-and-left movement of the bullet) and elevation (its up-and-down movement). With open rear sights—the ramp type with a spring-steel leaf and a notched elevator—however, windage adjustments are achieved by tapping the sight at the point were it joins the barrel, with

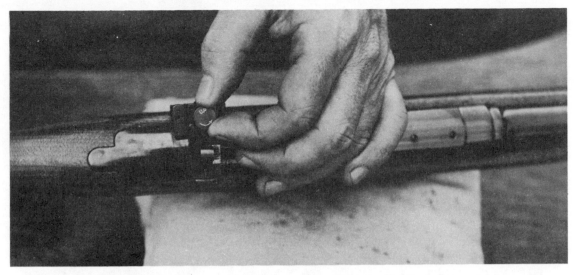

Windage and elevation adjustments on peep sights are controlled by screws.

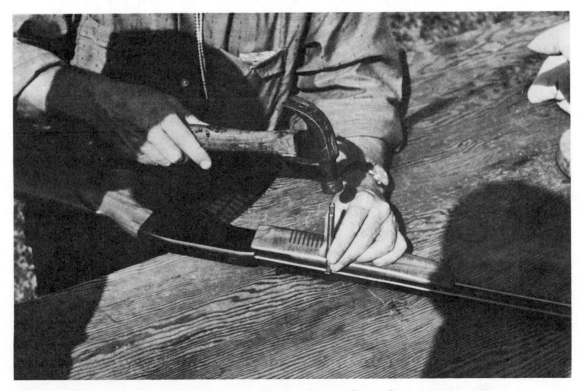

A hammer and brass or bronze rod are needed to make windage adjustments on some open iron rear sights.

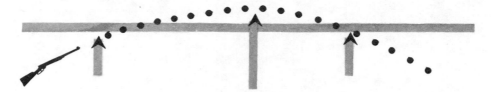

After leaving the gun, a bullet twice crosses the line of sight—once shortly after leaving the barrel and the second time, at a longer range, as it is pulled toward the earth by gravity. In between these points it will always be higher than the line of sight.

a brass or bronze rod (or even a wooden dowel) struck lightly by a hammer. Don't use a steel rod or just a hammer; it will mar the sight. Elevation is handled by the notched movable elevator which rides in a groove under the spring-steel tension of the sight leaf. Each notch is usually designed to handle one inch at 25 yards of range, but only experiment will prove out each adjustment. Elevation adjustments can be made on the spot, but rifles with open sights are generally sighted for windage when they are first fired; after that shooter judgment, "Kentucky windage," is used.

2. Learn how to adjust point-blank sighting to trajectory. A bullet travels in a parabolic curve after it leaves the barrel; it crosses the line of sight twice after being fired—once on the rise and once on the fall. (To compensate for drop, sights are adjusted so that the barrel points very slightly upward; the bullet doesn't defy gravity and actually climb, of course, but its curve does cross the straight line of sight twice as it travels.) Under optimum conditions, an arm of a given caliber will be at zero point on the target at, say, 26 yards and again at 230 yards. Sighted-in at 26 yards, this rifle is supposed to zero again at 230, and the mid-point between these two distances will find the bullet somewhat higher than the line of sight. To obtain the mid-range trajectory of any cartridge, check the factory ballistic tables on it at the time of purchase. Bear in mind that bullet weight directly affects the mid-range trajectory figures; a 110 grain load has an entirely different set of figures (closer to the line of sight at mid-range) from those of a 200 grain load in the same cartridge.

THE FUNCTION OF THE COMB

A telescopic sight, which eliminates the rear and front sights, offers a single unit set above the action and barrel of a rifle, requiring the shooter's

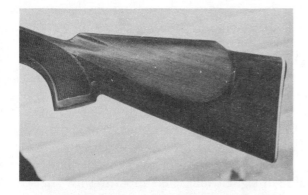

Here is the cheek rest on a rifle designed for shooting with a scope.

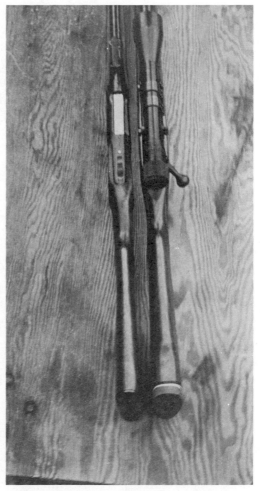

Note how much higher the comb is on the rifle at right; this added height aids in shooting a scoped rifle.

The added thickness of a comb, again shown on the rifle at right, also helps to position the eye for scope sighting.

line of sight to be about an inch above the barrel, depending on the model and mounting of the sight. With such a raised line of sight, it is obvious that the gunner's cheek must be placed higher on the comb of the rifle than is necessary with conventional sights. For this reason, stocks of rifles designed to take scopes may have two features that are not found in regular stocks: a built-in cheek rest and a higher comb—or in some cases a Monte Carlo stock.

The comb on a Monte Carlo stock is both thicker and higher at the point where "drop at comb" begins. The added thickness, combined with the cushioning rise of a cheekpiece, determines the position of the shooter's face, affording him a somewhat higher line of sight while still supporting his cheek. The *raising* of the master eye puts it into direct sight-picture relation to the sight itself.

The extra thickness and height of any comb regulates the line of sight with relation to the bore. If the comb is too thick (so that the master eye is forced to one side of the sight line), cross-firing may result, which means that the bullet hits on zero vertically but off zero horizontally. Thinning the comb and the cheekpiece will correct this. Conversely, if the comb is too thin, the master eye will approach the sight line from the far, or off, side. The addition of a cheek pad will bring the eye back into center on both stock and sight in this case.

MINUTE OF ANGLE

A minute of angle is the amount of movement in a rear sight that has the adjustment value of about one inch at 100 yards, two inches at 200, etc., in windage or elevation. (Micrometer hunting sights are usually set up in half minute "clicks," requiring the movement of two clicks per inch for each 100 yards; target sights have gradations of one-fourth inch for the same distance.)

SIGHT ADJUSTMENT WITH A SCOPE

The telescopic sight eliminates front and rear sights; it actually functions as the front sight although it is mounted at the rear of a rifle. With such a sight, bullet impact is controlled by windage and elevation screws either incorporated into the mount or set on the side and top of the scope and shielded by cap screws. Moving either the windage or the elevation dial shifts the bullet's point of impact accordingly. (In many scopes, this is a two click operation for one minute of angle—one inch of movement at 100 yards.)

Here is a telescopic sight made some years ago, with windage and elevation screws in the mount. Today the adjustments usually work internally, as in the scope below.

In most scopes, the adjustment screws are part of the instrument itself.

The movement of these dials controls the shift in position of the scope reticle or of the whole scope, depending on the rig's design. When the adjustments are internal, this movement is the opposite of the one employed for a rear iron sight setting: to move the impact point of a scoped rifle to the left, you shift the reticle screws to the right; to move the zero to the right, the reticle screws move to the left. For elevation, the screws moved up bring the impact point down, and the screws moved down raise the impact point. Not every scope works the same way, but in each case the direction is indicated on the dials or screws.

Chapter 4

HOW TO SHOOT TARGET RIFLES

The fundamentals of riflery become much more refined and more complex when the gunner takes up formal target shooting. In this game, only the highest degree of accuracy is tolerated. Top notch shooters, in effect, become testing machines for accuracy of both the rifle and the ammunition.

To achieve such a high standard of excellence, a definite training program must be established and maintained. Indeed, formal target shooting imposes such a high standard of physical performance and mental training that relatively few gunners have the dedication to carry on to develop into top ranking target riflemen. And it must be said that only for such dedicated marksmen will target shooting remain interesting. Many starters succumb to acute boredom from punching holes in paper. The fine target shooter must, initially, have a keen spirit of competition, or else the game soon palls on him.

Normally, in the first few weeks of intensive practice under good coaching, a beginning target shooter will build up his scores close to the "possible" level—i.e., 100 out of 100, or whatever the maximum happens to be. But from this point forward, steady gains are difficult to make, and here the dedication of the shooter determines whether he will keep on to develop X-ring performance or forget about the whole thing and be content to remain just a good rifle shot. The X-ring is within the 10-ring, the smallest area on targets. For instance, in a 100 yard competition, the black of the target is six inches in diameter; of this area, the 10 ring is two inches across; within this is the one inch X-ring, the circle that separates the men from the boys in target competitions.

In Chapter 2 we gave the rudiments of rifle shooting for beginners, using an extremely simple type of bolt action single shot rifle. The purpose there was to instill the basic elements of rifle marksmanship in the beginner, a knowledge that the rifle—at this stage—would perform beyond his abilities. But the formal target shooter is not so readily content with his rifle. He demands, and needs, a firearm and ammunition capable of the best accuracy,

The X-ring is within the 10-ring; it counts for 10 points, just as the 10-ring does, but when target shooters' point scores are equal, the man with the most X-ring hits wins. Most targets for formal competition have this X-ring, but some with small bull's-eyes omit it.

fitted with sighting equipment that can deliver this accuracy to the target . . . if the shooter does his part.

Any shooter interested in formal target work is virtually obligated to join a local rifle club, not only to obtain range facilities and to benefit from the knowledge and experience of old hands at the game, but to gain some preliminary notions about the type of rifle he will choose. Almost all such shooting groups have "club" rifles which are loaned to new shooters. After trying out a couple of different models on the range, the new shooter will be in a better position to make a decision on what target arm to purchase.

TYPES OF TARGET RIFLES

The rifle you will choose to start target shooting will in all likelihood be a single shot .22. It may be one of the dozens of moderately priced bolt actions that are available, or it may be one of the specialized target shooting rifles. Starting with a simpler arm and then trying out some of the more specialized ones before making an expensive purchase is the wisest and simplest way to determine what arm suits you best. A mass-produced, mod-

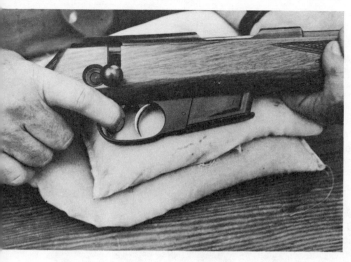

Set triggers are sometimes found on target rifles and varminting rifles. Pressing the rear one cocks the front trigger, and then the barest touch on the front trigger fires the rifle.

erately priced bolt action .22 is at the starting end of the scale. What is at the other end? The arms used by dyed-in-the-wool target shooters. In addition to specialized sights that we will come to shortly, there are such devices as set triggers. This is generally a combination of two triggers; the rear one usually cocks the front trigger, which in turn fires the arm. There is also a single set trigger that incorporates both functions—the setting, or cocking, and the firing; this type, however, is rare. The advantage of set triggers is that they are always adjustable; they can be set to a predetermined, extremely light release. But it takes considerable experience to use one of these devices effectively. The average rifle takes about five pounds of trigger pressure to fire, but set triggers usually work at about two. The danger for the inexperienced shooter, as you can see, is firing the rifle before he is ready.

Two other specialized rigs deserve mention to illustrate kinds of target shooting you might progress to. One is free rifle shooting, a primarily European style of competition that is used in many international events (the Olympic Games, for one) and is becoming better known in this country. It is perhaps the most difficult type of target shooting; iron sights are the only kind permitted, the bull's-eye of the target is much smaller than in American events, and the range is 300 meters. A special rifle, called a free rifle, is used. It is extremely heavy (maximum weight is 17 pounds, and most rifles approach this weight), it utilizes a palm rest that the shooter's left hand grips instead of holding the rifle's forearm, and, in competition, a sling.

Another style of specialized competitive shooting is bench rest. In this, the objects are to reduce human error to a minimum, and at the same time produce ammunition that brings out the best of each rifle's capabilities. Factory ammunition is therefore almost never used; rather, most of the bench

The free rifle, used most frequently in European or international competitions, is used in the most difficult of target events.

Bench rest shooting reduces human error to a minimum. These events are better tests of the rifle's inherent accuracy and the accuracy potential of the ammunition than of the shooter's marksmanship.

rest shooters make their own (all ammo is specially made, whether by the shooter himself or somebody else) and center-fire rifles are used, because ammo for them is the only kind that can be loaded without factory equipment. The rifles are fired from a fixed position, a shooting bench similar to the one we used in Chapter 2, and the forearm of such guns is extremely wide, being designed to rest on the sandbags of the shooting support for maximum steadiness. The shooter's hands and body generally do not affect the sighting or release of the shot. Bench rest shooting is done from 100 and 200 yards.

In all of these events, a single shot rifle is most often used, or if the shooter employs a rifle that holds more than one cartridge, he will generally operate it as a single shot—manually loading each cartridge before he fires. There are two reasons for this: first, most target shooters welcome the loading interval as a break from the concentration that is a necessary part of competitive target shooting; second, target shooters don't want to take the chance, no matter how small it is, of damaging a bullet as it is carried through a rifle's feeding mechanism. The only exception to this one-at-a-time rule among top notch target shooters is for military rapid fire events.

INDOOR SHOOTING FOR NOVICES

The novice target shooter will do well to begin his shooting program on an indoor range. At the short 50 foot and 25 yard distances, he will learn his first lessons in style, holding, "position shooting," and all the groundwork necessary to become a match shooter. He will also, after looking over the targets fired by club members, see the scores he is expected to make to hold his own in competition. Once he passes the hurdle of learning the proper positions used in indoor competition and can score well on the regulation targets, he will be better able to cope with the additional problems he must face in outdoor competition—ranges that may reach 1000 yards, varying light, wind drift, and mirage.

At the outset, the new target shooter should begin his practice in the prone position. A great many local and regional matches are held for this position only, and it is in the prone position that the top scores are made. Hence,

Indoor 50 foot or 25 yard target shooting is the starting point for beginners.

the prone shooter's rifle (whether he is a beginner or a veteran of formal competition) must be able to deliver the goods when loaded with the right target ammo and fitted with proper sights. As a matter of fact, some shooters have specially stocked rifles only for prone shooting, rifles that allow them to hold their heads more comfortably and see the sights more accurately and easily than with all-position target rifles.

IRON SIGHTS

Generally, it is best to begin match competition with iron sights, since these are basic in rifle shooting and, in any event, if you hope to become an all-around target marksman you *must* shoot with iron sights at times. Iron sights for today's target shooter are pretty much fixed in design, with apertures for both the front and rear sight. The latter has an adjustable iris so that the amount of light entering the sight, and its field of view, can be controlled. Opinions vary as to the best size of front sight aperture—as in most other equipment used by target shooters. Some experts prefer an aperture size that allows them to see only a faint ring of white around the black bull. Others, equally proficient, use an aperture large enough to cover the two outer white rings of a regulation target. Light conditions, range, bull's-eye sizes, and the shooter's vision play a part in this selection, and some experimenting must be done with different sizes before the ideal is selected. For indoor shooting, however, an aperture size of .135 to .145 inch is usually good. Outdoors, because of the difference in size of the sighting bull, a somewhat smaller size is preferred, about .120 inch. It should be obvious from this discussion that shooters using aperture sights at the front and rear of their rifles use a center hold (as opposed to the six o'clock hold that we talked about in Chapter 2, the hold that is most often used in field shooting

Here is a typical aperture rear target sight. The peep is on the right; the eye relief and adjustment screws are in the center portion of the photo.

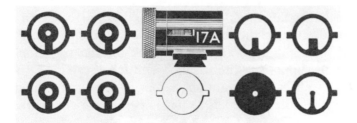

Target shooters' front sights are also apertures. The housing is the part with "17A," which indicates the model number, on its side. The other devices are interchangeable discs that regulate what the shooter uses in aiming—three widths and styles of post in a circle and various sizes of peeps that regulate how much of the target the shooter sees when aiming.

and the one that any target shooters who employ post or bead front sights also utilize).

However, these technicalities and choices in sighting equipment will not be troublesome to you, as a new shooter, until you have become proficient in the use of the various shooting postures, and there are, naturally, specific rules about these.

PRONE TECHNIQUE

Let's take the prone position as a starter, since this will be your first choice—and it is the easiest in which to score well—on the formal target range. The National Rifle Association's Smallbore Rifle Rule, ⚹5.6, states: "Prone—body extended on the ground, head toward the target. The rifle will be supported by both hands and one shoulder only. No portion of the arms below the elbows shall rest upon the ground or any artificial support nor may any portion of the rifle or body rest against any artificial support." This is all clear enough and gives the shooter some latitude in placing his body where he feels most comfortable. Generally, the angle the shooter's body takes to the line of fire will be from about 30 to 45 degrees, with the left elbow directly under the rifle to create the firmest support.

A properly applied sling, which we will talk more about in Chapter 11, is a must in all prone match shooting, for without it the shooter finds it difficult to relax, and relaxation is the key to consistent accuracy. The sling loop should be mounted high around the upper part of the left arm, with the left hand snug against the forward swivel. This relieves the necessity of the shooter gripping hard against the rifle's forearm with his left hand. The sling tension holds the rifle's forearm naturally and easily in the palm of his hand. In addition to the left hand now being easily able to support the rifle, leaving the right hand relaxed to work on the trigger pull, the right shoulder aids in supporting the firearm. Tension created by the sling keeps the rifle's butt well back in the pocket formed in this shoulder. Without a sling, the weight of the rifle tends to force open the angle of the forearm and

Here are the four regulation target shooting positions, from left to right: prone, standing or offhand, kneeling, and sitting.

At left is a target shooter in the prone position. He is wearing typical target gear—a shooting jacket with a padded right shoulder against which the rifle butt is placed, a pad at the bottom of the right elbow, and a target shooter's glove on his left hand to aid in achieving a steadier hold.
The standing, or offhand, position offers the least support for the body and the left hand. This shooter is not even aided by a sling, but his left arm is tucked in close to his body to help him steady his rifle.
The kneeling shooter is a left-hander. Note that he is sitting on his rear heel and that an instep pad is tucked under his left instep.
The shooter at right is using one of the variations of the standard sitting position. He has his legs crossed at the ankles; other shooters prefer their feet spread apart.

biceps; relaxed shooting under this condition is hard to imagine, especially when you consider that target rifles are heavier than any other rifles. The reason for this weight, by the way, is to provide shooters with rifles that won't waver when they're aimed at the target. A heavy rifle is a distinct advantage when accuracy is its only requirement and you don't have to carry it through the fields all day and make snap shots.

With the sling properly placed, the shooter's shoulders will be parallel to the ground. If the right elbow is too close to the body, the right shoulder will be uncomfortably cocked up in the air. To level the shoulders, simply move the right elbow away from the body. If, after getting into position, you find that you are not pointed directly at the target, simply shift the body slightly to the right or left, using the left elbow as a pivot, until the target lines up without muscular strain. A shooting glove on the left hand adds comfort by cushioning the hand against the sling swivel.

Once the sights have picked up the target, pressure on the trigger begins. Your right hand should grip the stock just firmly enough so that you can press the trigger without strain. Most shooters prefer to use the tip of the forefinger for contact with the trigger, but this will vary with differences in a shooter's hand size and a rifle's stock dimensions. The important thing is good, careful trigger squeeze—whatever part of your finger is doing the squeezing—and don't forget the "Magic V" that we talked about in Chapter 2.

Also important is the matter of a conscious "follow-through" as the shot is fired. This is fully as helpful as the well known swing-through with a shotgun which we will cover in Chapter 5, since it implants the idea of a careful, relaxed let-off firmly in mind. It also is helpful in "calling the shot" so that you will know exactly where your shot *should* have gone into the target. "Follow-through" also aids in preventing flinching or balking at the trigger. You simply determine ahead of time that you are going to keep on squeezing that trigger until the shot hits the target. It's more a mental state than anything else—but it helps scores.

Once you have achieved some proficiency with the prone position, you will go on to others, particularly in indoor shooting, where three position and four position matches are standard. The additional three positions are, of course, sitting, kneeling, and standing, or offhand; in all of these, trigger squeeze, follow-through, and the "Magic V" are of the same importance as they are in prone shooting.

SITTING

The sitting position is rather comfortable, and many shooters find that it is steady enough so that their scores compare well with prone shooting scores.

The NRA Sitting Position Rule, ✄5.8, states: "Weight of the body supported on the buttocks and the feet or ankles, no other portion of the body touching the ground. The rifle will be supported by both hands and one shoulder only. Arms may rest on the legs at any point above the ankles." Even though the rule doesn't specifically cover it, most shooters in this position have their bodies facing about 45 degrees away from the target, feet spread well apart, with the right elbow positioned against the inside of the right knee. The upper left arm rests on the left knee, with the elbow directly under the rifle barrel. A variation of this position is with the body lower and farther forward, the left knee almost into the left armpit and the right arm and elbow well within the right leg. Still another legal position is the "crossed leg," with the ankles crossed and pulled well in under the legs, and with the point of each elbow resting on the inside of each knee. It's up to you to decide which of these positions is the steadiest and most comfortable. The first position mentioned will do well for a starter.

KNEELING

The kneeling position is hardly any steadier than standing, and we will discuss it only in relation to target shooting. Here again the shooter has several choices of "legal" positions. The NRA rule, ✄5.10, states: "Buttocks clear of the ground but may rest on one foot. The rifle will be supported by both hands and one shoulder only. The arm supporting the rifle rests on the knee or leg. The elbow of the trigger arm will be free from all support. One knee must be touching the ground. A soft pad may be used if placed fully beneath the instep with the toes and knees touching the ground."

Many shooters sit on the inside of the right foot, although this is not comfortable for long unless a thick shooting mat is under it. On hard ground or a floor, when a pad is not used, the shooter rests his right buttock on his right heel, with the toe flat on the ground. If the instep pad, as mentioned in the NRA rule, is used, it is tucked under the right instep so that the toe touches the ground and the shooter sits on the back of the right heel. In any case, the position is rather awkward but must be learned if you are to shoot in four position matches.

STANDING

The toughest target shooting position is standing, or offhand. It is the most difficult from which to build good scores, and skill in offhand shooting comes only with unremitting practice. NRA rules offer options as to just what you can do in the standing position: whether you may use a sling or not, whether the left arm may be held close to body or not, and whether the hip may be used to support the left elbow. The rules change with different matches, so the various positions should all be learned and used in practice firing.

Since only the left arm supports the rifle in the standing position, considerable practice, both dry-firing and with live ammunition, is required to condition the muscles to the weight of the rifle. At the same time, keen coordination between trigger control and sight alignment must be attained, for at best the perfect sight picture is obtained only for a fleeting instant and the reflexes must be trained to let off the shot at precisely that instant. The synchronization between trigger let-off and precise sight alignment is far more difficult in the standing position than in any other—which accounts for the difficulty in placing bullets in the 10-ring when shooting offhand.

In using the two basic positions for standing (either the "off arm," with left arm extended to grasp the rifle's forearm, or the lateral "offhand," the elbow on the hip for a rest), the shooter's attitude is about the same with regard to the line of fire—almost 90 degrees off it. In using the extended arm hold, the left elbow is directly under the forearm, with the weight of the rifle supported mostly by the heel of the left hand. The right elbow is raised as high as is compatible with comfort, and the feet are spread about 12 inches apart, with the weight balanced equally on each. In the hip rest position, the shooter puts a bit more of his weight on the right foot by leaning slightly backward. The left arm is held snugly against the left side, elbow on hip; the rifle is supported by the extended and spread tips of the fingers and thumb from directly below. The right elbow is not carried quite so high in this position as in the off arm hold.

For best performance in the standing position, the rifle should be somewhat muzzle-heavy—which is the reason for the popularity of heavy barreled rifles for three and four position matches. The extra forward weight helps to steady the swing of the sights on the bull, and there will fo.ever be a swing of sights in offhand shooting, since no one can hold the rifle steadily on target.

There are several important points in making good offhand scores. One of these is perfect balance of the body with no muscle strain to either right or left. And deep, slow breathing is even more vital in offhand work than it is in the other positions. As the rifle is raised, take a long, slow breath; then as the sights come on target, slowly let air escape until the sights settle in the desired position. Then hold about half a lungful of air until the shot is squeezed off. If the shot can't be gotten off this quickly, lower the rifle and start over again. Don't try to out-hold your breath or hurry the shot simply because you are running out of air.

Another point in getting high scores in the standing position is not to hope for dead center let-offs with every shot. A good offhand shooter will tell you that the best scores are made not by getting off many dead center hits but by *not* getting many wide ones. A group of offhand shots into the nine ring will win more matches than a target with half a dozen 10s and the rest of the shots scattered out of the black.

OUTDOOR TARGET SHOOTING

Once you become proficient on the indoor range, you will move to the 50, 100, and 200 yard outdoor ranges in the course of regular match competition. The 200 yard line is the longest competitive .22 distance, but center-fire shooters sometimes look at their targets from 1000 yards away. At any of these long ranges, wind deflection and heat mirage compound the problems of trying to put your bullet into the 10-ring every time. The wind problem is highly important, since a fairly stiff cross wind can push a bullet out of the black even with a perfect center hold and correct let-off. How-

In outdoor target shooting, not only is the range longer than for indoor events, but the shooter must cope with wind and, frequently, mirage problems.

ever, there are no fixed rules about wind deflection—as you will discover on your very first day of outdoor long range shooting.

The initial procedure on a breezy day is to fire sighting shots on the non-record target, then adjust sights to compensate for the *average* drift. And here the key word is "average," for only the individual shooter can make judgments as to when the wind effect is "average" or plus or minus any amount. The feel of the wind on your cheek or the drift of smoke from a cigarette tossed ahead of the firing line will give you some insight, but what is happening over the entire distance between you and the target is extremely variable and its assessment rests upon personal judgment. Once your sights are set for the correct average wind drift, it is then up to you to employ "Kentucky windage"—holding off just a bit to one side of the bull or the other as the wind increases or lessens. Only years of practice and judgment will solve this problem.

Heat mirage is another variable in match shooting, and its effect is to make the target shimmer slightly over your sights. Most shooters check the effect of mirage (and sometimes wind drift when it is present at the same time)

This free rifle shooter is checking mirage, and possibly windage, through a spotting scope of 20X or more.

by use of a spotting scope of 20X or more. Mirage is vertical distortion; by looking at the target through the spotting scope, an experienced shooter can estimate the amount of this distortion. Then he will check wind drift, which has a horizontal effect on his shooting; he will ascertain the wind's force by seeing how fast the vertical distortion heat waves move horizontally. But you will learn these things from experience and from your shooting companions on the range. These are problems that must be faced when they arise, and their effects are so variable that no amount of compiled data covers each situation. So you can see that keen judgment, as well as top notch precision, make the polished match competitor.

Chapter 5

HOW TO SHOOT SHOTGUNS

The first time you fire a shotgun, you assume a brand new approach to the sport of shooting—and it takes thorough preparation to master. In a way it's easy, but this very simplicity is a tough concept for many shooters to grasp. There are two crucial points in the development of a shotgunner. The first, which was covered in Chapter 3, is adjustment to recoil; the second is the gaining of the ability to hit a moving target, which is the crux of firing a shotgun.

Temporarily, you must discard part of what you have learned about aiming a shoulder arm, for with a shotgun, unlike a rifle, *little conscious attention is paid to aim.* You'll learn, instead, fluidity of movement with this gun, and sacrifice some of the rigid control of rifle operation.

It is said that a man cannot be a good shot with both a shotgun and a rifle. He may be excellent at one and passable at the other, but he almost never excels at both. This dictum, though based on performance, can be disproved by adopting a *planned* cycle of practice. Excellence can be more easily attained by carefully following step-by-step instructions and continually repeating the fundamentals. Once you have made the big jump to instinctive shooting—the pointing rather than the aiming of a shotgun—you should reacquaint yourself with non-instinctive rifle control. Your goal is to familiarize yourself so thoroughly with both sets of movements that each of them becomes second nature.

WHAT IS GAUGE?

The width of a shotgun bore is traditionally measured in terms of gauge. This method was devised by gunsmiths many years ago, and has never been changed. Each numerical gauge designation specifies the number of lead balls the same size as the diameter of the bore that make a pound. Twelve spheres, the size of the bore of a 12 gauge gun, equal a pound; this is how the 12 gauge was assigned its number. The same is true of the other gauges—the 10, 16, 20, and 28.

The converse of this, to help clarify it, is that if you wanted to determine the gauge of a piece of tubing, you could cast a number of lead balls that exactly fit into the tube; the number of these that weighed a pound would tell you the gauge of the tube. The only exception to this rule of measurement is the .410 bore; this small shotgun bore is measured by caliber, just as our rifles and pistols are.

THE DIFFERENT TYPES OF SHOTGUN

As in rifle shooting, you must first understand the mechanism of the types of arm you are going to use. Shotguns come in five basic models—pump, semiautomatic, single shot, double barreled, and bolt action. Let's take up their differences in order.

PUMP: The bolt assembly of a pump shotgun, like that of a pump operated rifle, works by an action bar that moves the bolt backward and forward. This movement, executed with the left hand by a right-handed shooter, frees the magazine feed carrier arm within the action, allowing it to place a fresh cartridge where the returning forward action of the bolt can pick it up and seat it in the chamber.

The magazine styles in pumps are similar; they are all tubular, spring activated, and running under the barrel. Loading operations are also similar; you load through the port, which is on the underside of the receiver. Shells must be worked through the action to unload the arm in some cases, while in others a magazine release button permits unloading through the rear of the tube. Familiarize yourself with the process by loading and unloading a gun. Work the safety button (at the front or rear of the trigger guard in all but a few models) and notice how its operation resembles that of the safeties on big bore rifles.

SEMIAUTOMATIC: A semiautomatic shotgun action is much like that of a semiautomatic rifle. For the first shot, the bolt assembly must be hand activated—a shell is chambered and the gun is cocked. When it is fired, the gas that is formed is utilized to thrust back the bolt, eject the spent shell, cock the hammer, and pick up another cartridge from the feed slide as the bolt slams back into place under spring pressure. Safety features are also the same as on a rifle. And, as on a rifled arm, there is an action spring that closes the bolt assembly and that you must keep your fingers away from

Just as with the pump action rifle, pulling back the forearm of a pump shotgun extracts and ejects the used shell and cocks the gun; the forward movement chambers a new shell and locks the action.

You load shells into a pump shotgun through a port located in the underside of the receiver.

if you prefer them all in one piece. The loading operation is the same as for pump guns—but to be on the safe side, *never assume you know, always repeat*. Familiarize yourself with the gun, just as you did with the semiautomatic rifle.

SINGLE SHOT AND DOUBLE BARREL: With the single shot or double barreled nonrepeating shotgun, you meet an entirely different concept of gun action, one that breaks at the breech. This breaking is controlled by a hinging action at the base of the fore end and the forward part of the action. When the gun is open, ammunition is inserted directly into the chamber or chambers. The gun is locked into firing position at the rear by a spring bolt, which is controlled by a locking lever at the head of the tang. Double barreled models come in two popular constructions, the side by side and the over and under. In the latter, the barrels are placed one atop the other, incorporating all the principles of side by side operation while giving the shooter a single barreled sighting plane. The double is the safest shotgun action ever constructed. The simple process of releasing the locking lever (by pushing it to the right with your thumb) opens the action and lets you see if the gun is loaded. You can't discharge such a gun accidentally when the action is broken open—a good argument for its use by new shooters.

Virtually all double barreled, single barreled and over/under shotguns are controlled by a tang safety, a checkered sliding button at the top rear of the receiver assembly. A few foreign models have the safety on the side of the action housing or at the forward part of the trigger guard. In many models the safety is automatic, returning to the "non-fire" position each time the action is broken and closed. The only time an automatic safety does not operate is when the action is not broken after firing. In trap and skeet guns, an automatic safety is not necessary, since the gun is never loaded until the shooter is in position and ready to fire; in fact, the safety is nonexistent on some custom models. The safety button on most trap and skeet guns is thumb activated and nonautomatic, remaining on "fire" position during the reloading and closing of the action.

There can be no more important lesson for the newcomer to double barreled operation than to become ever aware of the safety and its "on" or "off" condition. Keep releasing the safety until it becomes a completely natural motion. If you forget to take an automatic safety off just before you shoot, the gun won't fire, and you may miss your chance at a fast moving target.

Most side by side and over/under doubles have two triggers, one to fire each barrel. In side by side models, the front trigger fires the right barrel and the back trigger fires the left; in over/unders the front trigger fires the bottom barrel and the back trigger the top one. In guns equipped with a single selective trigger, the barrel selector button is usually located on or near the trigger. By pushing this button to the right, you set the gun to fire the right,

Safeties on pump shotguns are usually at the front or rear of the trigger guard.

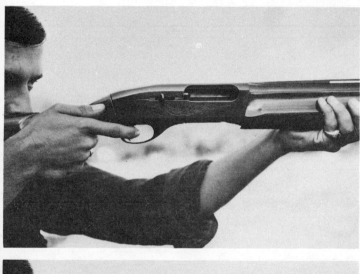

The bolt must be worked by hand for the first shot of an autoloader, but after that the gun works itself. Gas formed by the ignition of the shell is utilized to send the bolt backward as well as to move the shot charge forward. As the bolt moves to the rear, the used shell is extracted and ejected and the gun is cocked; then the bolt comes forward, picks up a fresh shell, chambers it and locks into position. All you have to do to fire is pull the trigger for each shot after the first.

The safety on an autoloading shotgun is generally the same as on an autoloading rifle—a button on the trigger guard.

You load a typical autoloading shotgun just as you do a pump model—through a port on the underside of the receiver, just in front of the trigger guard.

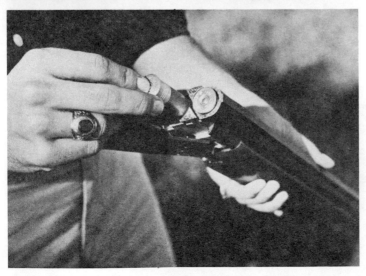

Single barreled single shots and all double barrels—both side by side and over/under—break open at the breech. To load these guns, you insert the shells directly into the chambers.

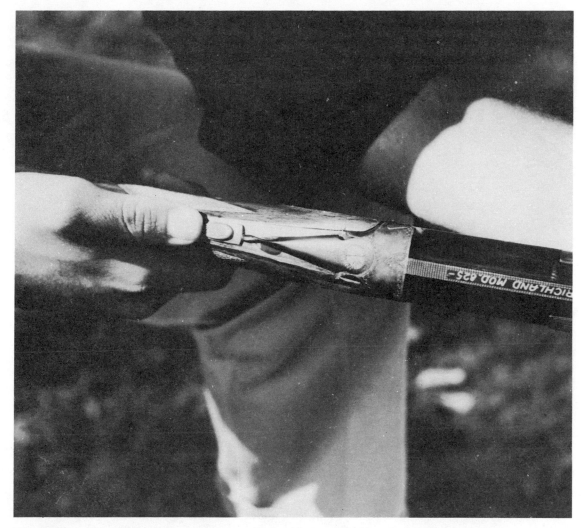

The locking lever, shown above the shooter's thumb, is pushed to the side to open the gun. The tang safety, the sliding button on which the shooter's thumb is resting in this photo, moves backward and forward to the usual "fire" and "non-fire" positions. On many single trigger models, side to side movement of this button regulates which barrel fires on the first pull of the trigger.

or the bottom, barrel first; by pushing it to the left, you set it to fire the left, or the top, barrel first.

Several popular foreign made over/under shotguns, like the Browning Superposed and Winchester 101, use a selector system that is integral with the safety. These guns each have a top tang safety latch exactly the same as the one shown above, but it can be switched to the right or to the

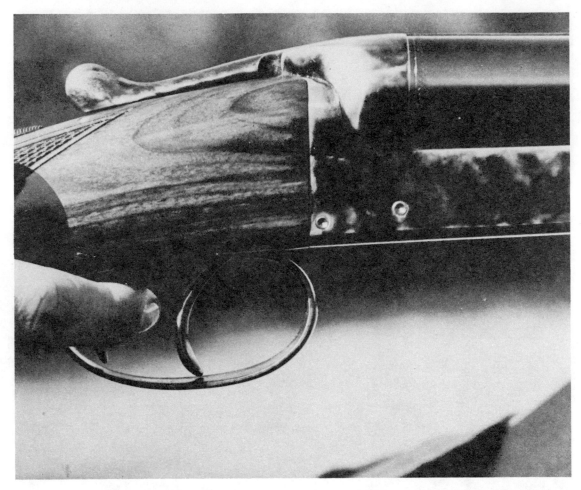

Many double guns have two triggers, one for each barrel. In a side by side, the front trigger fires the right barrel; in an over/under, the front trigger fires the bottom barrel.

left to change the order of firing. The positioning of the latch clearly indicates the barrel that is ready to fire; the letter "O" marks the latch stop for the top barrel and "U" is the position for the bottom barrel.

Some single trigger guns don't offer a choice of which barrel you may fire first. In these, with a *non*selective single trigger, the first pull will always fire the right barrel on a side by side or the bottom barrel of an over/under; the second pull discharges the left, or the top, barrel.

Some double barreled models feature automatic ejection—spent shells are thrown out of the chambers when the gun is opened. Others only extract;

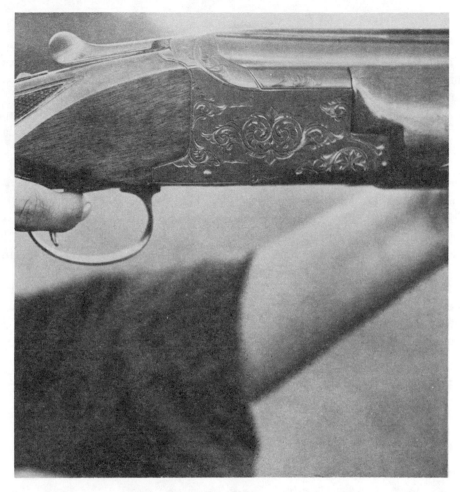

Some double barrels have only one trigger. If that trigger is "selective," you can flick a button that determines which of the two barrels will fire first. If the trigger is "nonselective," the first pull of the trigger fires the right, or the bottom, barrel.

they break the fired shells loose from the chambers, pushing the empties part of the way out, and the shooter must manually remove them from the gun.

BOLT ACTION: This type of single barreled shotgun is operated the same way you operate a bolt action rifle. Extraction, ejection, and the chambering of a fresh shell are accomplished by manually working the bolt. Economy models often utilize bolt operation, but many shooters object to this design because of the slowness involved in getting off a second shot. Shells are usually held in a removable magazine.

SHOTSHELLS

A shotgun shell is an amazing engineering feat when all its components are considered. To understand what happens when you pull the trigger, take a standard plastic shell and examine its parts.

At the top is the crimp, through which the shot charge breaks upon firing. The crimp is an extension of the case, which used to be made of laminated paper; most shells today use a plastic case. In the "pie" crimp, a common type, the top of the case folds inward in sections which meet at the center—just like sections of a pie. This crimp gives the shell a flat top. Some paper shells are topped by a flat wad, held in place by a rolled crimp.

Note the shot itself. These tiny round pellets vary in number and size, depending on the particular load. Because they tend to be deformed as they are pushed through the barrel, a protective plastic collar is sometimes wrapped around the shot. This improves pattern density.

Next come the thick filler wads which separate the shot pellets from the powder charge. And then the third wad—cup shaped with its concave side facing the base of the shell—forms a gas chamber to seal the bore and prevent gas from leaking forward past the shot charge it is supposed to propel.

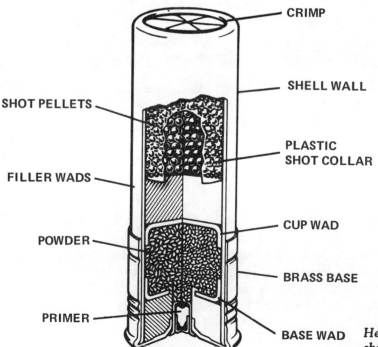

Here is a cross-section of a shotshell, showing each of its parts.

In many shells, the waddage and protective collar are combined into one plastic piece. Various combinations of cardboard, felt, cork, or other materials may be used in the wad column.

Now you will see the powder, which comes in various types. Burning speed, for example, differs just as it does in rifle and pistol powders. All types, however, are modern smokeless powders; the dram is the standard unit of measure, but it serves only as a yardstick since charges are actually weighed in grains.

Below the powder is the base wad, and then comes the brass base, containing the primer, which is the key to the firing cycle. In an opened shell you can see the exposed unfired end of the primer and visualize how the hot flash of this component ignites the powder, which in turn converts to gas, exerting sufficient pressure against the cup wad to drive it and the two paper wads and the shot charge through the crimp and along the barrel, emerging as a killing load.

FUNCTION OF THE CHOKE

Most of us have handled a garden hose. In the process, we learned that constricting the nozzle makes the water shoot out in a tighter, more concentrated stream; the smaller the opening through which the water must pass, the narrower and more concentrated the stream. A shotgun choke operates on much the same principle. It has the effect of creating greater density in the shot pattern at a given range. Constriction, therefore, controls the size of the target area hit by shot and, conversely, the amount of the charge to hit within a given area. It does *not*, however, increase range the way a tightened hose nozzle does.

Choke on most shotguns is obtained by constricting the barrel, usually within the last four inches of its length. Gradations of choke run from cylinder bore (no choke whatever) to super-full (the maximum amount of constriction). These built-in tightenings of barrel diameter determine shotgun pattern. For all single barreled guns, adjustable choke devices are also available; they are fitted to the muzzle and can be changed from shot to shot.

Although the installation of a variable choke is a job for a gunsmith, its operation is simple. Most such devices consist of a short metal sleeve, marked with choke settings. You determine the degree of choke by turning it to the desired setting, just as you would turn a garden hose nozzle. Another available type incorporates the use of interchangeable choke tubes, each with a different constriction.

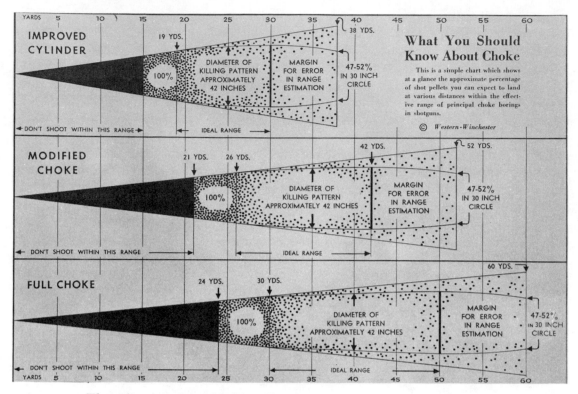

These diagrams show the different percentages of pattern effectiveness at various ranges for each of the three most common degrees of choke.

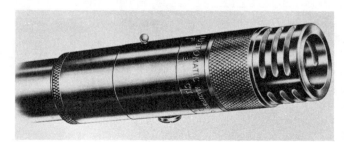

This is what a sleeve-type adjustable choke device looks like on the end of a shotgun barrel. You simply turn it to the desired setting.

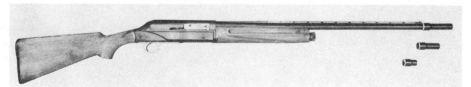

Another type of choke that can be changed is this one that utilizes interchangeable tubes, each of which gives a different degree of constriction.

WHAT IS PATTERN?

When shot emerges from a shotgun muzzle, it does not do so as a unit. Rather, it comes out much like water from a hose—in a string, measuring from seven to 13 feet in average 12 gauge loads. The constriction applied to this shot string by the choke determines the density of the pattern—that is, how many pellets hit within a given area.

After a shot charge travels a short distance, from the gun's muzzle, this string takes the general shape of an ice cream cone, traveling wide end foremost. The degree of choke controls the size of this wide end; it is measured by the percent of the shot charge that strikes within a 30 inch circle at 40 yards. In a cylinder bore, the pattern density is about 40 percent (in other words, 40 percent of the pellets strike within the 30 inch circle). However, in full and super-full constrictions, this pattern density jumps to an amazing 70 percent or more at the same 40 yard range. In some guns, the combination plastic wad column and shot collar in many of today's shells may actually produce densities of 90 percent.

No two barrels will pattern the same way. One shotgun may favor ⚡7½ shot fired through its 28 inch barrel with a modified choke, but may not handle ⚡6 shot as well. The number designation indicates the size of each pellet; the lower the number, the bigger the shot. Action of the pellets against the wall of the barrel and against one another causes a certain amount of flattening and distortion of the outer pellets in the charge. Because of this distortion—called deformation—these pellets will not fly true. On emerging from the muzzle, they wander, and may fall well outside the patterning area. Only trial on the range will indicate which load your gun handles best.

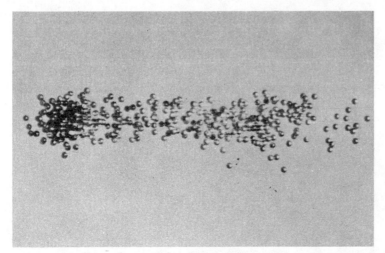

Shot does not emerge from the muzzle of a gun as a unit; rather it comes out in a string, and its length increases as it moves farther from the gun.

MOUNTING THE SHOTGUN

Now we deal with the massive differences between the average holds for a rifle and a shotgun. The latter is always shot offhand (rather than from a prone or sitting position), and we shall point out where the pitfalls lie in this type of shooting.

The shotgun must be mounted in one fluid motion; you release the safety as the gun comes up, bring the gun against the shoulder, and pull the trigger as the target comes into view over the barrel—all in one uninterrupted movement. The left hand is used to guide the gun as it swings with the moving target; the right hand keeps the gun seated firmly against the shoulder, and the trigger finger slaps the trigger—instead of squeezing it as with a rifle or pistol.

The shotgun is brought to the shoulder in a fluid motion called mounting. When this is properly executed, you propel the barrel toward the target, throwing it forward and up into position in one movement, releasing the safety at the same time, then seating the stock against your shoulder and, finally, pulling the trigger as the target comes into view over the barrel. Unlike the rifle hold, which requires your muscles to be braced, the shotgun demands a combination of relaxed speed and coordination of eye and hand.

IMPORTANCE OF THE LEFT HAND

The piano player whose aptitude lies only in his right hand is not a good piano player. The same applies to a shotgunner. To be good, you must make full use of your left hand. This is the key to the smoothness of swing and the maintenance of the proper lead that indicates a polished shooter.

The left hand, or fore end, grip is a cradling of the gun in the hollow formed by the cupping of the hand, bracing the barrel and fore end between the thumb and four fingers. The fingers and thumb *do not wrap around* the barrel, but rather ride along it in a cupped position. The left arm should be as nearly straight as is comfortable. Unlike the rifle hold, which dictates that the elbow be bent and directly under the firearm, the shotgun hold permits muscular extension. Get your left arm well out for better control and gun swing.

THE RIGHT HAND'S GRIP

We described (in Chapter 2) the "Magic V" grip in rifle handling; this must now be modified, for where the right hand rifle grip stresses control and squeeze, the shotgun grip does not.

On a shotgun the right hand lies well back on the stock, clasping the pistol grip firmly with the last three fingers and leaving the index, or trigger, finger free. The index finger curls over the trigger of a single trigger shotgun. With double trigger models, the ball of this finger touches the front trigger, allowing the shooter to drop back to the other trigger after firing the first shot with a minimum of effort and a maximum of speed. The thumb position is not critical; it can rest parallel to the tang or wrap over it, whichever is more comfortable for you.

In firing a shotgun, you slap the trigger instead of squeezing it as you do with a rifle. The error, or barrel waver, caused by this jerking of the trigger is compensated for by the width of the pattern.

HEAD POSITION

As a rule, the first mistake any student makes in mounting a shotgun is to place his cheek on the stock by tipping his head to one side. Properly, the head follows the barrel's direction, moving forward toward the target with the barrel. When mounting the gun, as the barrel rises and comes into line, your cheek should move forward to meet the comb of the stock at the moment the butt plate makes contact with your shoulder. This movement can be clarified by saying that your head *drops forward* to meet the rising comb.

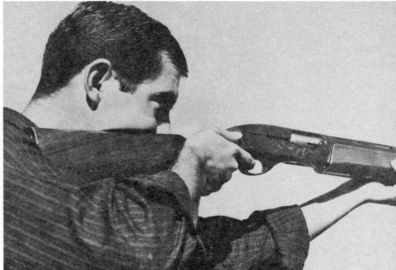

The head must follow the line of the barrel. There is no sideward movement when you correctly place your cheek on a shotgun stock; rather you drop your head forward to meet the comb.

SHOULDER POSITION

As the shotgun seats itself against your shooting shoulder, the shoulder line of the body is approximately 45 degrees off the line of fire. This off-center approach is caused by the extension of your left arm and the cupping of your right shoulder to form a hollow for the butt.

UPPER BODY POSITION

During the free swing of shotgun firing, the upper body from your waist to the top of your head literally follows the barrel toward the target. There is a definite forward movement of this section of your anatomy, leaning slightly into the gun and toward the target. Avoid the common fault of tensing the stomach muscles. As in golf, the pivot is all-important in a shotgun swing, and it is aided by this relaxed forward movement.

The basis of good shotgunning is complete freedom of movement. Your arms and upper body form a bent "Y" to perform the shooting act while your legs are nothing more than a relaxed shooting platform supporting the entire operation. Never tense your muscles, for *rigidity destroys swing* and, at the same time, accuracy; moreover, it amplifies recoil. Bear in mind that a 12 gauge shotgun has more recoil than 90 percent of our current big bore rifles; staying relaxed to ride with it is the way to overcome its effects. With the forward position of the upper body compensating for the sudden strain on the abdominal and back muscles, the recoil is absorbed effortlessly.

FORGET THOSE FEET!

It would be a great thing if people could forget that they have feet and legs while they're shooting shotguns at game birds. This may not be true of skeet and trap, but nothing disturbs a new shooter more than thinking about where his feet are at the moment of firing.

Because the upper body performs the entire act of shooting a shotgun, no solidity of stance is required—a strange experience for one accustomed to the constant bracing and control that are needed to hold a rifle steady. Try to realize that if you are relaxed, you can aim, fire, and hit your target—even though you're standing with your feet crossed! By ridding your mind of worry about foot position early in your wing shooting career, you will simplify the job considerably. For the sake of safety alone, you must look ahead rather than down, and learn to take your feet for granted, as you do in walking.

THE EYES AND POINT OF AIM

Remember that with a shotgun you do not have to be directly on target as you do with a rifle. Where a single bullet must be directed with minute care and accuracy, a shotgun load is pointed at the target, taking into consideration the margin of tolerance offered by its pattern—30 inches at 40 yards. In other words, you can be some 18 inches to the right or left of your target and still score a hit—although perhaps a marginal one.

Shooting a shotgun at a target is no more than extending your finger and pointing it at an object. The shotgun is simply an extension of that finger and is pointed in the same way. Just as you could not point accurately with one eye shut, you keep both eyes open in shotgun shooting for two reasons. First, you have far better peripheral vision with two eyes working for you; second, your judgment of target range and speed is much more accurate. In the case of a right-handed gunner, the right eye is the "master eye"—the one directly behind the breech—in a majority of cases. But although a shotgun does have a bead front sight, it is best overlooked for a long range approach to good shooting. The moment you start consciously lining up that sight with the target, you lose your fluidity of swing and instantaneous ability to point the gun. All you should be conscious of at the time of firing is the barrel out in front of your eyes tracking the target, not the bead sight.

SHOTGUN FIT AND ITS EFFECT

None of us are built alike, and physical variations affect our shooting. Some people have short arms, requiring a shorter than standard stock, combined with less drop at heel and comb. Conversely, a tall person with long arms needs more drop at heel and comb and a longer stock.

The person of average build can shoot factory stocked guns. These usually come in the following measurements: drop—2 to 2½ inches at heel, 1⅛ to 1½ inches at comb; stock length, 14 inches.

To understand the principles of stock fit, it is a good idea to learn these fundamentals:

1. Drop at comb and heel is measured by laying a ruler along the barrel and extending it back above the stock. The distance between this horizontal line and the top of the comb is drop at comb. The distance between the ruler and the top of the butt is drop at heel.

2. The comb controls both the horizontal and the vertical position of the line of sight from your eye along the barrel to the muzzle.

3. The heel controls the vertical angle of stock and barrel.

When you mount a strange shotgun for the first time, several possible angles of sight exist, all controlled by the fit of the comb. Here are some typical ones:

1. You are looking directly over the barrel (comb correct in width and height).

You can check shotgun fit by having a helper stand six feet away. After making sure your gun is empty, mount it and point it at his right eye. If it fits correctly, your eye will follow the line of the barrel to his eye.

2. You are looking over the barrel, but your eye approaches the line of sight from the left for a right-hander (comb right height but too thick).

3. You are looking directly over the barrel, but seeing its full length (comb right thickness but too high).

4. You see the full length of the barrel from the left of the line of sight (comb too thick and probably too high).

5. You see only the breech end of the gun (comb too low, and possibly too much drop at heel).

In short, *the comb is the most important factor* in fitting a shotgun to a shooter. The easiest way to find out whether or not a shotgun fits you is to do the following, after checking carefully to be sure your gun is empty: have a helper stand six feet away and facing you; mount the gun normally and point it at his right eye; have him look down the barrel and check your eye and face alignment over the sighting plane. If the fit is correct, your eye will automatically follow the barrel to his.

Certain adjustments can be made without taking wood from the stock or radically altering its shape. If the stock is too short, a leather or rubber recoil pad or boot may be attached to provide more length. If the comb is too narrow, a cheek pad may be added. Any other adjustment involves correction of the stock itself, which calls for the services of a stock maker.

"LEAD" AND WHAT IT MEANS

Many of us delivered newspapers when we were younger. If we owned a bicycle, we soon found that in order to hit a front porch from a moving bike, we had to throw the paper where the porch wasn't. This is the first rule of "lead." Briefly, lead involves figuring how far in advance of a moving target a gun must be aimed (and fired) so that the charge and the target will occupy the same space at the same time.

Nothing is more difficult for the average person to master than the art of gauging distance. For example, it is not easy to figure out from across a room how high the window sill is from the floor. Similarly, trying to measure out three feet, six inches ahead of a moving target from a distance of 30 yards is almost ridiculous. Therefore we shall not attempt to teach lead in feet and inches, but rather in terms of target lengths and the sight picture as it appears to you.

Back in the days of market gunning for waterfowl, one of history's truly legendary duck shots made his mark. A wealthy amateur, Fred Kimble was a dedicated duck and goose hunter, so proficient that he could beat the market gunners at their own game. Yet for all his skill with a shotgun, Kimble had a basic principle of lead that, if applied to my own shooting, would ruin me forever as a waterfowl shot. It worked for him because it conformed to his own *sight picture* of a correct lead.

Shooting at a 40 yard range, Kimble figured he had to lead a crossing duck one body length. Should that same bird be crossing at 60 yards, he lengthened this lead to three body lengths. Taking the same bird at the same yardage but from a quartering angle, he would divide his lead by two.

My own picture of lead is vastly different, but getting down to fundamentals and away from theory, correct lead is nothing more than the movement of the barrel through the line of the target's flight at the speed of the target, passing it and pulling the trigger while *maintaining target speed* with the barrel. If the picture that works for you is to lead that bird by seven body lengths, so be it. The mental picture is perfected through practice; it cannot be taught. But the idea of barrel swing and follow-through can be.

These are the basic barrel positions you must use to make a kill on the given target positions:

▶ Target straight away—hold dead on.
▶ Target straight away and rising—hold over.
▶ Target straight away and falling—hold below.
▶ Target rising and moving left—hold high and to the left.
▶ Target rising and moving right—hold high and to the right.
▶ Target moving away and falling left—hold below and to the left.
▶ Target moving away and falling right—hold below and to the right.
▶ Target crossing—hold ahead.
▶ Target incoming—hold ahead and continue the swing ahead.

Study this list until you have a thorough grasp of these fundamental deflections. It will simplify later corrections and instill the beginning of a sight/ lead picture in your mind.

We have mentioned body length of targets because this is a good way to estimate lead and range. Just remember that you must lead the same distance for a teal as for a goose if each is passing you at the same speed 35 yards away. Your mental picture of lead may have been nine body lengths on a 12 inch teal and only three body lengths on a 36 inch goose, but the total measurement of lead was the same (in this case nine teal or three geese would measure about 108 inches, showing that you wouldn't lead one more than the other). Also remember that these examples are arbitrary. You will only find your best lead picture through practice.

To hit a moving target with a shotgun, you must pick up speed and direction, swing through, fire, and follow through—in this order:

1. Track the target with eye and gun barrel.

2. Starting with the barrel behind the target, swing through as you find its speed and direction.

3. As the barrel passes the target, set up your sight/lead picture while maintaining target speed and direction; having established this, fire.

4. As you pull the trigger, consciously maintain your sight/lead picture, exaggerating the follow-through if necessary until the bird starts to fall.

PRACTICING WITH CLAY TARGETS

There is a saying that nothing succeeds like success. Among other things, it applies to learning how to shoot. When you can see that you are improving, you are encouraged to greater efforts.

Even when you feel that you have gained sufficient proficiency in mounting your shotgun to your shoulder, do not try to run before you can walk. Set up a stick 20 yards away and hang a standard clay target on it. Insert a single shell into your gun and try to break that clay target with instinctive gun pointing procedure—mount the gun, find the target, and pull the trigger all in one fluid motion. When you find that you can do this consistently, it's time to move on to the flying target from a hand trap.

Have a companion gently lob clay birds with a hand trap, as straight away from you as possible. As you become more adept, have him increase the target speed as well as the angle of deflection. After each miss, ask him to point out what mistakes you made during the execution of the shot, and then get him to try to duplicate the target angle on his next throw.

You will discover quickly that you must get on the target as soon as possible, i.e., while the flight of the clay bird is on the rise. Once it passes its

A good first target for a beginning shotgun shooter is a clay target set on a stake about 20 yards away. The gun should be mounted smoothly, the target sighted over the barrel and the trigger pulled all in one motion.

peak of momentum, it begins to drop rapidly and this will be confusing at first, since to break a dropping bird your hold must be well under it.

As your first lesson in shooting at a moving target will be essentially the same as in shooting at the stationary clay bird hung on the stick, you should be shooting only at dead straightaways thrown from the trap. Your goal at this point will be to get on target fast, cover it, then fire—all in a smooth movement of gun handling. It is too soon at this point to be concerned about leading the target. Getting the gun up quickly and breaking the bird is the important factor. Then, as your shooting speed improves, your target thrower should throw you faster targets, but still keep them in a straightaway path, high enough for you to see them readily against the sky.

Then, after you can break these straightaways, shot after shot—but not until then—are you ready for some lessons in leading the bird. If you are a right-handed shooter, you will find it easier to make your first angle shots at clay birds thrown from your left side, provided always that you are keeping

The hand trap that throws clay targets is the next step in learning shotgun shooting.
The first clay birds should be hurled as straight away from the shooter as possible.

both eyes open as you pick up the bird's flight, track it, and shoot. Your target thrower should stand no more than 10 feet to your left, to give you a slight right-quartering angle. Again, you will shoot as quickly as you can get on the bird, but you will now find that you must swing a bit ahead of it (to its right side) as you fire and follow through with the swing. Try leading this target by about twice its width, a bit more than eight inches. If you get on and fire quickly enough you should break it every shot.

At this stage, you will probably discover that you are stopping the swing of the gun as you pull the trigger. This is a natural reaction since it was not necessary to consider follow-through when you were shooting at straightaways —no more so than when you were breaking the clay birds hung on the stick. But now you must be conscious of that important follow-through—the left hand keeps moving the gun until after the shot is away; otherwise your lead will be lost.

The explanation of this phenomenon—and you will begin to think of it as

After the hand trap, move to a fixed practice trap. This device, which must be firmly anchored, is similar to the hand model except that it throws the clay birds farther and faster. The fixed trap fires when the helper pulls a lanyard attached to the trap.

a phenomenon when you miss several easy targets in a row—is a matter of simple mechanics. The firing of the gun and breaking of the target combine several elements of elapsed time, each in itself insignificant, but which add up to enough time to allow the clay bird to escape the pattern. Your eye initiates this reaction when it signals the brain that the gun is pointing just far enough ahead of the moving target to compensate for its forward movement. Your brain reacts to this by signaling your finger to pull the trigger. This takes about two-tenths of a second if your reaction time is normal. When the trigger is released, the lock time of the gun (the time from trigger release to cartridge ignition) must be added to the total. This varies in different guns, but it averages about one-hundredth of a second. The cartridge now fires and drives the shot out toward the target. This will take about one-fiftieth of a second before the load reaches the clay bird. By adding up these little increments of time and dividing them into the speed of the bird, which often reaches 50 miles per hour for a hand thrown target, it is easy to see that it will move several feet along its flight path from the instant your eye signaled correct lead until the shot pattern intercepts that path. It thus becomes vitally necessary to keep the gun moving throughout this rapid action sequence of events if you are to maintain the amount of lead you had decided was correct to begin with. It sounds complicated, but really it is not if you keep your gun moving throughout the entire act of firing.

Once you begin to break the slight quartering angle clay birds, you will progress to shooting at sharper angles until you reach the final step—birds that cross at a right angle to your line of fire. And you will note quickly that as the angle increases you must increase your lead proportionately. Often on right-angle crossing shots at a range of 25 yards, you will be leading the bird as much as a dozen of its lengths, over four feet. However, it must be repeated that only *you* can determine this amount of lead for each of the various angles. Your reaction time, and to some degree your gun's lock time, are the variable factors that make it impossible to set up a schedule of exact figures for leads.

As you gain confidence with a shotgun and are breaking a heavy percentage of clay targets thrown from a hand trap, switch to a fixed practice trap, which gives your target speed and control that can't be obtained from a hand model. Again, ask to have your errors pointed out and try to correct them. Bear in mind that repetition is the key to shooting proficiency. You may get impatient, but in the process you will learn to shoot.

Chapter 6

HOW TO SHOOT TRAP AND SKEET

Shotgun mastery is a thrilling achievement, but perfection takes practice. If this practice can be enjoyable as well as profitable, so much the better. The sports of trap and skeet shooting are competitive gems; they bring about that hard-to-come-by familiarity of a man with his gun that can only be accomplished by firing hundreds of rounds.

Our grandfathers grew up during an era of extremely heavy game population. It was an age of magnificent shooters, and though the names of Ad Topperwein, Fred Kimble, and Annie Oakley may mean little to the younger generation, their exhibitions and competitions were as much of a box-office attraction as baseball and football games are today. While no shooting "stars" exist in modern times, there are two large bands of clay target shooting adherents—members of the National Skeet Shooting Association and the Amateur Trapshooting Association. They and their many target shooting companions in this country call "Pull!" on some 150,000,000 clay targets each year.

To grasp the intricacies of these two sports, you should be taught each separately, and great emphasis should be placed on the fundamentals.

WHAT IS TRAP?

Perhaps the greatest boon to firing at clay targets in the United States was the banning of live pigeon shooting a few decades ago in all but a few states. To take the place of pigeon shoots, a substitute called "trap" became popular. Named for the trap release used to hold live birds during the heyday of pigeon shooting, it was a game that originated in England in 1720.

A trapshooting field might best be described as an open area terminating in an arc where the shooters take up their positions. At the center and 16 yards forward from these positions is the trap house, from which clay targets

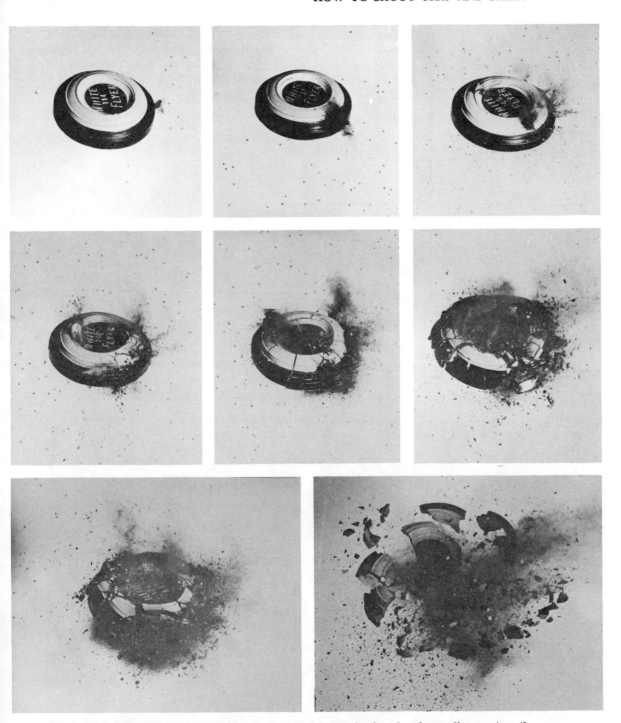

These high speed photographs show a clay bird being broken by shot pellets as it sails through the air. The pictures also illustrate what we said earlier about shot string—that the entire charge of shot from a gun does not arrive at the target at the same time.

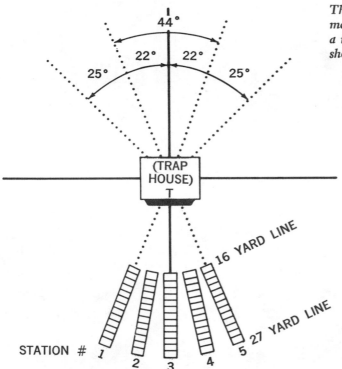

The drawing shows trap field angles and measurements. The photo with it shows a trap squad on the firing line, with the shooter at station #3 taking a shot.

are propelled by a spring activated arm. This arm, or trap, is designed to throw a circular clay target measuring 4 5/16 inches in diameter and 1⅛ inches in height, weighing within five percent of 3½ ounces. The target must be thrown a distance of no less than 48 nor more than 52 yards through any angle up to 94 degrees from point of issue, and away from the firing line. This means that the bird can take any angle up to 47 degrees right or left of the center line.

The firing line arc is vertically divided by five walks at three yard intervals, each marked out in measured shooting stations. The forward line of each walk is exactly 16 yards from the trap house, while the rear line is usually 27 yards from it. These distances, used in competitive handicap shooting, determine the degree of difficulty for the shooters.

For the purposes of instruction, we shall deal with the forward or 16 yard line only. From left to right, facing the trap house, are five shooting stations, #1 through #5. Behind the shooting line is the release and scoring shack where the referee keeps score and releases the targets.

THE TRAP GUN

In Chapter 5 we dealt with basic shotgun shooting. We used a fairly open bored, lightweight field gun as a teaching arm. We also discussed choke and pattern, A trap gun presents a different appearance from a field gun; it has a long 30 or 32 inch full choke barrel (although some trap guns can be ordered with less choke to counterbalance the ultra-dense, tight patterns of modern shells) and its stock is high at the comb and straighter than its field counterpart. As you will see, there are good reasons for these differences. The majority of trap enthusiasts use pump guns, although other actions are permissible; trap models usually have a solid or ventilated sighting rib atop the barrel, and 12 gauge is the standard bore size.

The average clay target thrown from a trap house is broken by a charge no larger than 3¼ drams of powder propelling 1⅛ ounces of #7½ shot; the optimum range is 32 yards—figuring that the gunner is 16 yards from the target when he calls for it and tracks it an additional 16 yards before the actual breaking. Usually, however, the clay bird is slightly more than the optimum 32 yards away when hit, making full choke guns helpful.

Field shooting is as different from trap as taking a crack at a running deer with a .30/06 would be different from shooting the same rifle in a bench rest match. Trapshooters are "set" shooters in that they have the gun mounted and cheeked, their feet solidly and precisely placed *before* calling for the target. As there is no need for speed in assuming the shooting position, the shotgun used in trap has a higher and thicker comb than a field gun. This

The gun at left in this photo is a trap gun, with a stock much higher and straighter at the comb than the field model at right.

would slow the shooter down in the field or whenever he had to mount the gun immediately before firing it, but it insures that he will keep his eye accurately aligned over the sight rib on the trap range and it helps to minimize the effect of recoil.

THE TRAP STANCE

Unlike the shotgun stance used in the field, the trapshooting stance seems awkward to the beginner at first, but once learned, it has the precision of stability and hold that produces results.

In Chapter 5 we said that your body takes the shape of a bent "Y" when you mount a shotgun. In trap, this "Y," formed by your arms and upper body, is exaggerated. Classic field form puts the shoulders off the line of fire some 45 degrees, but in trap this angle is lessened considerably, the shoulders coming around almost perfectly square with the line of fire. Some shooters use a completely square shouldered stance which, viewed for the

The trap shooting stance is with the feet about 12 inches apart and the shoulders almost square with the line of fire. With this stance, you will automatically lean forward, and this allows you to pivot to track the target and comfortably handle recoil.

first time, has all the grace of an ice skating elephant. But the score sheet shows "how many" rather than "how," and hits are what count. Now, having squared your shoulders with relation to the gun, you must position your feet with relation to the most extreme possible target angles. These angles determine the direction you face as you prepare to shoot.

Since targets are thrown at unknown (and unpredictable) angles in trap-shooting through an arc of more than 90 degrees, your stance at the different stations becomes important. For example, at station ✳1 you are likely to catch a bird thrown to an extreme left angle, 45 degrees or more from your shooting position. You must therefore be in position to take this bird if it happens to come in the five bird sequence thrown while you are at this station. The best system is to point your left foot at the spot you hope to break this extreme left angle target. If you plant your feet with the trap house as your center point, you will be "body-blocked" when the sharp left angle bird is thrown and you will not be able to swing with it easily. This is the bird you will inevitably shoot behind.

The same situation applies when you work through the stations to ✳5. Here you will often get an extreme right angle shot so you must anticipate this by pointing your left foot at the spot you will break this target. For right-handed shooters, this is the toughest angle on the field, since it is not as easy for a gunner to swing to his right as to his left. If you position the left foot with regard to the most difficult angle you are likely to get at each station, you will never be off balance when these sharp angle birds appear.

Take your position at the station, spread your feet about 12 inches apart and stand at about a 45 degree angle with the rear of the trap house. Now, shoulder and cheek your gun. Two things will become immediately apparent: first, with this squaring of shoulders, your eye naturally falls over the barrel; second, square as you are, you must lean forward, automatically setting yourself into a perfect shooting platform position to handle the twin difficulties of pivot and recoil. Such precision of position, while of course not practical in the field, operates in exactly the same fashion that it does with a target rifle —it eliminates waste motion and solidifies the stance, improving accuracy.

BREAKING YOUR TARGETS

Field shooting a shotgun is a matter of pointing; in trapshooting, however, you must be more precise. To be sure, the same principles of swing and follow-through still apply, but here the barrel is consciously aimed from the beginning of the shooting process. Trap does not call for great speed of hand and eye, but rather coordination and precision.

The clay target that sails so tantalizingly away from you is doing two things by the time the average shooter's reflexes catch up with it—escaping and falling. Regardless of the flight angle it takes from the trap, and regardless of your position on the firing line, the target is always moving away from you and often falling by the time you cover it. Quick shooters take the bird at its crest or on the rise instead of waiting for it to fall, but the average gunner does not have fast enough reactions to accomplish this. Unlike live bird shooting, in which the target is usually rising in its attempt to evade the hunter, in trap you will find that you usually must hold *under* a clay target as you lead it.

High scores in trap depend largely on the speed with which you place the barrel on the target. The longer this takes, the farther away the target will be when you pull the trigger. The rules of the game allow you to mount and cheek your gun before you call for the target to be released, and if you know where to point, you'll gain a split-second edge.

Just where the gun should be pointed while you are waiting for the bird to appear is another problem. The gun muzzle should be kept below the point at which the target will appear so that its flight is always in your field of view without the gun barrel blocking any part of it. From station ※1, it is helpful to point the gun at the lower left hand corner of the trap house as you call for the bird. At the ※2 station, pick a spot about halfway between the left corner and the center of the trap house. At station ※3, aim your gun directly at the center of the trap house; at station ※4, point halfway between the center and the right hand corner of the house; at station ※5, you will aim at the right hand corner of the trap house. With this in mind, you will have less movement to make to get into a smooth swing, and you will be able to pick up the flight of the bird as soon as it appears. But remember—at no station should you hold the gun muzzle higher than the top of the trap house.

When you call for the bird, be sure both eyes are open and that you are scanning the field just in front of and above the trap house. Then, your peripheral vision will instantly pick up the bird and establish its line of flight before you commit yourself to swing on it. If you concentrate on a particular spot, anticipating a given angle, the bird may get away from you if it sails off at a different angle.

Pick up the bird over the barrel, track it and pass it, pull the trigger, and follow through, maintaining swing and lead. And remember: hold slightly *under* on every lead!

TRAPSMANSHIP

Trap is shot in squads of five gunners, each shooting from all five stations on the line, five rounds per station—a total of 25 birds to the string. With four other gunners on the line with you, certain safety precautions are mandatory, as are certain rules of conduct. Observing them makes the sport fun; disobeying them can turn it into a nightmare.

1. When not firing, stand with your gun open at the action, unloaded, and muzzle down.

2. When the gunner immediately before you in firing rotation calls for his bird, slip a shell into the chamber of your gun but do not close the action. The action is closed *only* immediately before you mount and cheek the gun.

3. Call for your target in a loud voice, using the word "Pull!" Avoid grunting, shouting, growling, or any other of the voice sounds some gunners emit when they try to appear seasoned. And realize that for the target to be released instantly, the referee must hear you.

4. After firing, eject the spent case from your gun immediately if the gun

doesn't do it automatically. Nothing disturbs the next shooter more than the sound of a shell being ejected just as he's set to call for his bird.

5. When your turn comes, be ready. Don't drag!

6. Trap—especially competitive trap—is not a talkative sport. Keep quiet, keep up, and reserve comment until the round is completed.

7. When you change stations, do it briskly.

8. Do not second-guess your shots—or anyone else's!

9. If your gun malfunctions, point it toward the outfield until you clear up the trouble.

WHAT IS SKEET?

Unlike trapshooting, which evolved into its present form over many years of various shooting games with the shotgun, skeet was deliberately created to fill a need for field shooting practice. William Harnden Foster, editor of a now-defunct outdoor magazine in Massachusetts, originated the idea of providing all the various angles a field shooter would encounter by laying out a shooting field in the form of a clock, with the birds thrown from a trap positioned at 12 o'clock to pass over the six o'clock station. These targets were fired at from each of the 12 hour positions, two shots from each position, with the 25th shot fired from the center of the circle at the incoming bird. Since this full circle arrangement presented danger to the immediate area of the skeet course, the game was modified to a half circle with traps at either side, and in this form was introduced to the public in 1926 by *National Sportsman Magazine*. A prize offered by the publication for a name for this new sport was won by a Montana woman who offered "Skeet," the English spelling of a Scandinavian word for "shoot."

Skeet differs from trap in several ways. To begin with, there are two trap houses rather than one. These are referred to as the "high" or left hand house and the "low" or right hand house. Rather than five shooting positions, a skeet field has eight, laid out in a semicircle. Seven of these stations lie on the perimeter of the semicircle; one, #8, is centered between the trap houses. The flight paths of all the clay birds thrown in skeet, those from the high house and those from the low house, intersect over the center post, five yards out from station #8. That is, the targets are not thrown along the diameter of the circle (or the edge of the semicircle), but rather they angle slightly away from the shooting area.

Another important difference is that trap operates on the principle of unknown target angle, while skeet uses a fixed angle—with the target pursuing the same path each time the trap arm is released. Therefore it is easy to see that skeet can be mastered by practice, even without instinctive ability. While

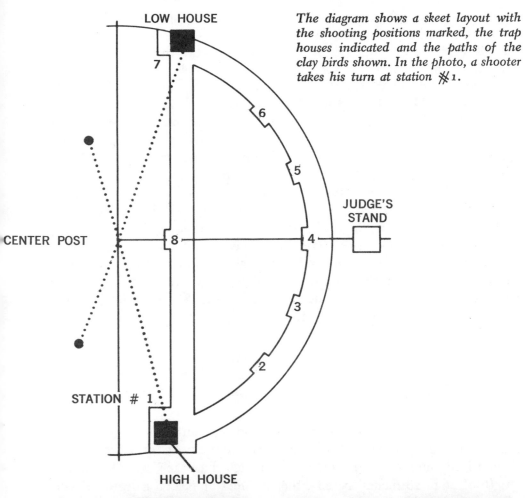

The diagram shows a skeet layout with the shooting positions marked, the trap houses indicated and the paths of the clay birds shown. In the photo, a shooter takes his turn at station #1.

the target angles are known, however, the angles of the shots vary more widely than in trap because the positions of the shooter change more radically. Skeet, for this reason, gives a much greater latitude of practice than trap for the gunner who wants to use this sport to sharpen his field shooting eye. Skeet shooting, in fact, offers almost the same variety of angles that you will find in the game fields. But while it provides a wonderful way to keep a shooter sharp in the off-season, its inherent predictability means that even though a shooter is excellent at skeet, he may not be nearly as good against birds.

Skeet employs an "optional bird"—a shot that you repeat after you have made your first miss of the round. For example, if you miss the #4 high house bird and have been "straight" to this position (not missed any), you call for that same bird again to use up your optional shell. In the happy event that you complete all 24 targets without a miss, you may call as your optional shot any bird you choose, to attain the highest possible score for a round— a straight run of 25. You shoot two birds at each station, released one at a time (a total of 16 singles), then you shoot doubles, targets released from the high and low houses at the same time, at stations #1, #2, #6, and #7 (eight birds); this, with the addition of the optional target, gives you the total of 25 for each round.

THE SKEET GUN

Whereas trap is a long range sport (32 yards and farther), skeet takes close range shooting (4 to 22 yards). The choke requirements of a skeet gun are diametrically opposite those of a trap model. The skeet gun has a barrel length of 26 or 28 inches, bored either cylinder or skeet (a degree of choke affording very wide expansion of pattern at short range). There is usually a solid or ventilated sighting rib to give the gunner a faster sighting plane. The stock is standard, showing little or no variation from field gun stocks. Pumps and autos are preferred. Skeet competitions are held in four classifications: all gauge (in which the 12 is most often used), 20 gauge, small gauge (meaning the 28), and sub-small gauge (the .410). Until you have achieved some proficiency, the 12 gauge is your logical choice.

In its infancy, skeet was a game of speed and fluidity, based on the idea that it would improve field shooting. At first, the stock had to be held at elbow height when the shooter called for a bird, but as time passed, this purity of purpose degenerated until now a skeet shooter may (and almost all of the dedicated ones do) mount and cheek his gun as does a trapshooter. While in a sense this defeats the original purpose of the sport—to improve the field shot—it has created an advantage that the expert can magnify in "straight" runs.

This skeet gun has a ventilated sighting rib, which offers the shooter a quicker sighting plane. The rib is popular on guns for all shooting sports, not just skeet. The ventilated type is particularly well liked for sports such as clay target shooting, in which weight (or the lack of it) may be important, and even more important is the dissipation of heat waves rising from the barrel after much shooting.

Two shot sizes are favored by skeet shooters—#8 and #9. These are used for an obvious reason: small shot sizes, with many pellets to the load, offer high pattern density with open bores. In 12 gauge models these are usually 2¾ or three dram loads, since shot range is unimportant and the elimination of recoil and flinch is desirable.

THE SKEET STANCE, BY STATION

Unlike trap, skeet takes into consideration all sorts of shooting angles—straightaway, quartering, full crossing, overhead, and incoming. On all but the last, your target has had the opportunity to start falling, so you must hold under and ahead of it.

Since the ability to pivot is vital in skeet, relaxation of shooting stance is its most important requisite. You set your feet and mount your gun before calling for the target. You must anticipate where you're going to break the bird. Knowing, as you do, the path of its flight, it's simply a case of deciding what you will do. At any station except #4 and #8, one target will be outgoing and one incoming; whether it's the high or low house bird depends on the station. Study the diagram to help you remember which is which. At #4 you take both birds crossing; at #8 both are incoming.

In general, it is a good system to plan the breaking of each bird in the singles round as it crosses the center of the field. This, in time, will teach you a fixed amount of lead on each bird from each station. In doubles, this

A shooter at station #1. His target is the high house bird.

Station #1: with the low house bird as the target.

Station ※2: trying for the low house target.

system is not practical except for breaking the first bird, which should always be the outgoing target. You will still have time enough to break the incomer, or second bird of the double, if you break the first bird over the center. Now for a round of singles:

Station ※1. Your feet are placed about eight inches apart, knees and muscles relaxed. For the high house bird, place the muzzle of your gun at a 45 degree angle and keep your face raised slightly off the comb. In this way you will be able to see the bird a shade sooner as it comes from behind and above you. Sight the target over the top of the muzzle to compensate for target drop—and fire.

At every station, place your feet the same way, so that your heels are about eight inches apart. Some shooters prefer to move their feet from shot to shot, but this tends to confuse rather than help a beginner. Except in the case of station ※8, which will be covered in a moment, your left foot points approximately toward the spot where you want to break the bird. Some gunners keep their feet parallel, but you may find you're more comfortable with one foot forward, in a modified boxing stance.

To hit a target coming in from low house, track and cover the bird at nearly point-blank range as you fire. Don't forget to follow through.

Station ※2. The center of a skeet field is marked by a stake driven into the ground. This will be an important reference point, helping you estimate distances from the trap houses. For either the high or the low house ※2 bird, assume your stance with the barrel pointing about 14 feet along the track the

Station #3: the high house bird is the target.

Station #4: aiming for the low house bird.

*Station #5: the target is
the high house bird.*

bird will take from the trap house exit door. Cheek and mount your gun, call for your target, track, fire, and follow through.

Station #3. Pick up the high house bird about 12 feet from the trap house door, swing, and fire. Bear in mind that as the target's deflection angle increases, your lead should be proportionately lengthened. Because the angle of deflection is so great for this low house target, it takes the longest low house quartering lead on the field. You must follow through in a pronounced fashion to break this target consistently. Pick up the bird about 12 feet from the trap house door.

Station #4. All you need to know about the high and low house birds from this station is that the lead is long and the follow-through mandatory. Try to break the bird near the center stake. To do this, you should pick it up about halfway between the center stake and the trap house.

Station #5. The reverse of station #3, this is the longest high house quartering lead on the field. Pick up the target about 15 feet from the trap house door, swing through, and fire, breaking the bird at field center. The low house bird comes from your right, beginning its rise behind your field of vision. Pick up the bird 10 feet from the trap house door and break it at field center.

Station #6. The deflection angle diminishes on this high house bird. Pick

Station #6: the shot is for the low house bird.

Station #7: aiming for the high house target.

Station ☒8: these photos show the shooter's stance, tracking, and breaking of the high house bird.

up your target between the high house and the center stake and break it between the stake and the low house. The low house bird should be picked up 10 feet from the trap house door; plan its breaking point at or just past field center.

Station ☒7. Handle your incoming high house bird as you did the incoming low one at station ☒1—ride it into point-blank range and cover it on firing. The low house bird on this station is the only "no drop" bird on the field, for you break it before it crests, aiming directly at it. Plan to break this low house bird just before it reaches field center.

Station ☒8. This, the hardest shot of all for the beginner, is most often missed because the shooter lets the bird get a split-second advantage over him after his call; he is behind at the start and stays that way. At this station, the stance varies radically. Your toes point about 45 degrees to the right of the high house for its bird, and the same angle to the left of the low house for

Station ⚹8: note the stance of the shooter before he calls for the low house bird, and note also over what area of the field he breaks his bird.

that target; in each case your feet are about eight inches apart. Standing sideways, shoulder and cheek your gun at a 45 degree angle, aiming directly out from field center. Just before you call, swing the muzzle around and place it at the lower right hand corner of the high house door. When you sight the bird, swing up and cover it, shooting point-blank, but *continuing a swinging follow-through*. After shouldering and cheeking your gun for the low house target, point the muzzle at the lower left hand corner of the trap house door. Swing up on sighting, breaking the bird point-blank with a swing and follow-through.

Once learned, station ⚹8 is an automatic shot, rarely missed by seasoned gunners. Placement of both muzzle and feet, however, is very important, since you arc trying to gct the jump on your target.

SHOOTING THE DOUBLES

After completing your singles circuit of a skeet field, you return to station ⊁1 for the first of four sets of doubles—two birds thrown simultaneously, one from each trap house. The doubles stations are ⊁1, ⊁2, ⊁6, and ⊁7. You handle these birds exactly as you did in single delivery except that you *always break the outgoing bird first*. You break the high house bird first on stations ⊁1 and ⊁2 because it's the outgoing one; for the same reason, you take the low house bird first on stations ⊁6 and ⊁7. Remember to take one bird at a time. Break your first, then swing to your second. If you do this, the presence of two targets in the air will not be too disconcerting. It's legal to break the incoming bird first only if you declare your intention of doing so; if you accidentally break both targets with one shot (as they cross), you must repeat your turn.

SKEETSMANSHIP

1. Never load your gun until you are on station and facing away from the rest of your squad.

2. If you're shooting a double barreled gun or over/under with automatic ejectors, turn slightly away from the line so that you won't shower the other gunners with empty shells.

3. When you're on deck (next to shoot), stand about five feet behind the man on station and be quiet. Save all conversation until the end of the round.

4. Do not give unsolicited advice and do not "post-mortem" your own—or anyone else's—misses.

5. Call for your bird with a loud, clear "Pull!" And remember, the high house bird is always taken first.

6. If your gun malfunctions, keep the muzzle pointed toward the outfield until you clear up the difficulty.

Trap and skeet are games, and should be treated as such if you are to become a well-rounded gunner. Unless you plan to go into competition, limit the time you spend at them to the period needed to polish your skill. These two sports afford tremendous enjoyment, and they are aids to the field shooter —but not crutches.

Chapter 7

HOW TO SHOOT SMALL GAME, UPLAND BIRDS, AND WATERFOWL

Once your groundwork in handling and shooting the shotgun has been established successfully, you are ready to take to the field or marsh for some live target shooting. Here you will encounter every possible variation in handling a shotgun, and to gain a high rating in this department it will help much if you have spent time on the skeet and trap field which you learned about in the last chapter.

Rabbits and squirrels, in terms of numbers bagged, rank high on the shotgunner's game list, but each is a rather easy target compared to the flying game we'll be after. If you have familiarized yourself with the elements of lead and have mastered the concept of follow-through, these furred animals won't present any great problem. We would even venture to say, having taught many people to shoot—and then to hunt—over the years, that success will come easier against rabbits and squirrels than any other shotgun game. It's the flyers that present the challenge.

Remember that small game usually doesn't run quite as fast as birds fly, so your lead can be a bit less. Rabbits and squirrels are, of course, shot with small bore rifles—or pistols—as well as shotguns. When using a rifle or handgun on such game, you should restrict yourself to still shots if the game is more than 30 yards away. Therefore, lead is hardly involved, and the technique is the same as for other rifle or pistol shooting. A .22 rifle is the right arm for such animals up to about 75 yards (with a scope sight if you're going to take many long shots). Pistol range is usually limited to about 50 yards.

Just as trap and skeet shooting offer two distinct varieties of gun handling and shooting methods, you will find that wild bird shooting divides into two classes: upland game and waterfowl. And, although trap and skeet will broaden your skill with the shotgun, it takes years of field shooting to produce a top shotgunner, since the flight of birds is completely unpredict-

A covey of quail rises from typical cover close to a pair of hunters.

able—in the distance from which a bird may flush, in its angle of departure, and in its speed. Waterfowl are shot at many different distances, and each shot you take will be slightly different from those you have already made.

Now, just as skeet has taught you to handle a gun quickly for the shorter upland ranges, shooting regulation trap has taught you the more precise gun pointing demanded of a good waterfowl gunner. Each is a different field of effort (and you will probably be doing each with a different gun) involving on the one hand extremely fast mounting of the gun and instinctive pointing (skeet . . . if you call for the target with your gun at elbow level); on the other hand, more deliberate placement of the gun to shoulder and cheek, with a bit more time taken to establish accurate leads (trap).

UPLAND BIRD SHOOTING

Shooting quail is probably the most typical example of true upland bird shotgunning. These are small targets, fast on the getaway; when breaking from the ground cover in a covey, they offer several choices of target, each with a slightly different angle. To make "doubles" (two kills) consistently on these covey rises, you must be fast with a gun and, more important, make an instant judgment as to which birds to take out of a flock.

The temptation on a covey rise is to take the bird that is closest to you as your gun hits your shoulder. This is the obvious and easiest shot—if you are only after singles—but the smart doubles shooter knows enough to take a first bird from those that are the farthest away (if they are still within range) and save the close bird for the second shot. Here is just one instance where quick judgment is demanded in field shooting.

The element of surprise, which comes as the bird or birds move from the ground unexpectedly and often noisily, usually confounds the new upland bird shooter. As often as not, he gets a case of "the buck" and does one of two things: he shoots too fast, almost before the gun touches his shoulder, or he waits in stunned silence until the bird is out of killing range before he remembers he is carrying a gun. Neither reaction collects game.

For the novice, the roar or buzz of flushing wings is indeed unnerving. He usually complains that "he didn't have a chance to get his gun up." Actually, if the birds flush within 15 or 20 yards, he has plenty of time to put gun to shoulder, pick a bird up over the barrel, make his swing, and fire. The beginner also complains that a skilled bird shooter "snap-shoots" without taking time to point the gun accurately and swing with the bird—that this takes years of practice which he lacks and can't hope to gain quickly. Again, none of this is true. An accomplished bird shooter might appear to "snap-shoot" without aiming at the bird, but in reality this rarely happens. He simply goes through the whole sequence so rapidly and smoothly that he *appears* to snap-shoot, although he has picked up the bird's line of flight and calculated the amount of lead he needs to drop it as he brought the gun to his shoulder.

Although the novice gunner is startled by the flush of the bird, the veteran shooter puts this to his own use. The noise triggers the reflexes that get his gun into action; quite often his body will react in the proper direction even before the bird is seen, particularly in heavy ground cover. The trick is to move your left foot toward the *sound* of the bird (if you do not yet see it), which in effect aims your body in the proper direction even before you begin to mount your gun.

Furthermore, the good shooter will *never* begin to shoulder his gun until he *knows* the direction the bird will take. This means, of course, that he locks his eyes on the bird as soon as it comes into view, tracks it as it breaks away, and *never* takes his eyes off it until it is hit. There is not enough time, after the bird is spotted, to place gun to cheek and look down the rib or barrel, and then try to determine the bird's flight path.

In addition, if you look at any part of the gun—breech, barrel, or front sight —you will not then have time enough to shift your vision to track the bird and make the proper swing. Your eyes *stay on the bird* and you mount the gun, point it, make your swing to get your lead, then fire and follow through. Once your eyes and mind have committed you to this sequence of action, it is difficult to change it while the bird is still within killing range. In other words, you make your mental commitment as to just what you will do *before* you mount the gun, then follow through the act of shooting without being conscious of the front sight or the gun muzzle. Your eye will see the muzzle out of focus, but you will still make the alignment without actually looking at it or the front sight. If you miss the first shot, you will still be in a position to recover from the recoil and make another swing and lead for a second crack at it. The quick, skillful use of the second shot is the hallmark of a polished wingshot, best exemplified when he makes both shots count with "doubles" on quail, grouse, or other game birds.

All of this means that your handling of the shotgun must come as second nature, which does not happen readily if you only shoot on the regulation trap or skeet field under present day practices. The old "gun down" rule of skeet *did* help a great deal in teaching a novice how to handle a shotgun, but this art is rapidly fading except as it is personified by the veteran upland bird shooter. In field shooting, the gun must be handled as though it were part of your body and the act of mounting, pointing, and firing it must be just as natural and easy as pointing your finger at an object. In fact, this is exactly the way a good upland gunner shoots—just the way that anyone points his finger at a sign, a rock, a tree, or any other object he wants to designate to an observer. He watches the object with both eyes, throws up his hand with finger extended, and lines up on the object without consciously looking at his finger at any time.

You will find, as you develop smooth, relaxed gun handling, that the operation, like pointing the finger, becomes a natural movement that can be done speedily. You will no longer be convinced that a fast upland gunner is a "snap-shooter" who does not aim, or in more exact words, point his gun. This is the key phrase in shotgunning—"point the gun"—since a good wingshot does not aim.

In shooting upland game, a good pointing dog is a great aid. Not only does he find the game for you, but his point will give you a fair notion as to its location even though it is hidden in heavy ground cover. You will then have time to "get set," with gun ready to mount and your body facing in a favorable position. You will also be able to anticipate the moment of flushing as the handler, guide, or your shooting partner steps in close enough to make the bird flush. None of these valuable aids is present when you hunt upland game without a dog, which is a tough way to fill a game bag.

Without the dog, you must be continuously on the alert for the noise of the rising bird, and your reaction time must be hair-trigger if you are to put the gun on such a bird in time to down it. Nothing we can say here will help much in this connection. You are on your own from the moment you step

The English pointer, one breed of pointing dog, is frequently used for quail hunting.

into the field and you must be prepared to get off a fast, directed shot at any moment of the day. That this takes skill in gun handling is to put it mildly, for a high average of kills in proportion to the ammunition used is a great rarity in this type of hunting.

Grouse shooting is without much question the most challenging of all upland gunning. These birds—I am referring to ruffed grouse though there are other varieties—are masters at concealment and at the art of surprise. They leave the ground with a thunder of wings and, often, a scattering of dead leaves, to make a rapid exit through timber or brush. You simply do not get a good look at a ruffed grouse after he flushes except on rare occasions—and then he seems to put on an extra burst of speed.

Some gunners claim that quail or woodcock shooting is even tougher. I disagree. A quail is slightly smaller but not quite as fast or erratic in flight. A woodcock is still smaller and has an even more irregular, often corkscrew, take-off. But, again, a woodcock doesn't have quite the speed of a grouse and it is often shot at a bit closer range.

A ruff is almost completely unpredictable in his manner of leaving the ground and taking flight. He is just as likely to flush from almost directly behind you as in front, and more often to your right or left. He will buzz

Ruffed grouse provide the most difficult of all upland bird shooting. Their speed, their ability to conceal themselves, and the wooded country in which they are hunted make them very elusive targets.

off in flat flight, almost parallel to the ground in heavy timber, or will tower almost straight up in heavy, tall second growth. In between these extremes he gives you every variety of gunning angle. He quite often flushes out of dark, brushy haunts where light is dim and his somber garb of feathers blends well enough into woods background so that he is difficult to see. Compounding all this is his amazing ability to dodge and dart through heavy cover with undiminished speed; he is expert at putting a tree trunk between himself and the gun just as you pull the trigger.

Whatever you know about slinging a shotgun you will have to put to use each time you hunt grouse. If there is a rule, it is this: shoot at every bird that flushes within killing range. Only in this way will you learn to get your gun on one quickly enough to make kills. You will use a second shot more often in grouse hunting than for any other upland game except possibly quail, and

A retriever—in this case a Weimaraner—is a great aid in grouse hunting.

it is discouraging but true that you will also make more second shot misses than in hunting any other bird.

It is always good policy to swing on the bird and fire your quick shot even if he gets into screening cover. I have killed many a grouse that I did not see as my gun went off, only knowing I had scored when I heard the plump body hit the ground or saw a puff of feathers drifting down to mark the fall of the bird. Unfortunately, you will lose a fair percentage of crippled birds unless you have an expert retrieving dog, since a grouse seeks a hiding place even with his last breath of life. I have hit numerous grouse heavily with two shots, dropping the bird solidly and yet failing to find it even after seeing loose feathers on the ground where the bird struck. A grouse can go quite a distance if its legs are not broken, and it will find a hiding place under a log, a flat rock, or creeping vines if it has one ounce of energy left. This is tragedy, of course, but it is the inescapable pattern of grouse shooting. Realize, however, that the better you become with your gun, the more clean kills you will make.

Many times I have been asked, "How many feet do you lead a grouse?" which is something like asking, "How long is a piece of string?" Even if I were conscious of lead lengths in terms of feet and inches, advice would be meaningless, since no two shooting situations are exactly the same and lead lengths vary from shot to shot. Even when we talk about lead in terms of feet and inches in parts of this book, we do it to standardize our units of measure—a pheasant's length being quite different from a grouse's. In practice you will translate these feet into lengths of the bird you're shooting at. This is much easier than measuring foot-lengths in mid-air and something you will automatically do in time. Furthermore, even if I could mark off feet in front of a bird darting through the air, it would be of little use to another shooter. No two people have the same reaction time, and my three foot lead would not work for you if you need four feet. Actually, a fast shot does not require much lead on a grouse. These birds are usually shot at fairly close range (if you're to see them) and the quick swing of the gun on a fast shot usually cuts down the amount of lead you need—or think you need—by carrying the muzzle past your target, even though you may not realize it.

This probably sounds confusing, but only much shooting practice on upland game birds can establish your own pattern. Much of this has to do with the way the shot is made. For example, if you get off a rapidly swung shot at a grouse in heavy cover, where you are *forced* to swing and shoot as fast as you can, you will not take as much apparent lead as if you were shooting a cock pheasant out in the open where you have more time. This is true even if the range is the same and the bird is moving at the same speed and angle. When you have more time, you make a slightly more deliberate swing, which is slower, and thus you need more lead. I know one expert grouse gunner who says that he does not lead these birds at all. And this could be true since he is a fast and deadly shot. He apparently pulls the trigger as he covers the birds and lets the forward movement of his gun continue so that he gets the necessary lead. This is, however, no trick for the novice, who must experiment with different leads at different angles until he finds his own pattern.

Obviously the gun *must* point ahead of a moving bird to compensate for its forward flight, and this movement will not only be forward on a horizontal plane, but upward or downward, too—as when a grouse takes off from the top of a white pine. Here the gun must be swung—literally pushed—ahead of the bird's flight line in *both* directions: ahead and above or below. It is always wise to shoot a gun that throws its pattern above the barrels, since many, if not most, of your shots at any upland birds will be when they are rising from the ground and you are forced to shoot above them to connect. The high shooting gun automatically compensates for most of this upward movement in flight unless the bird really towers, as grouse and woodcock often do in tight, fairly high covers.

As you can imagine, there is no time for studied calculation in shooting upland birds in heavy cover. A glimpse of the bird is all you get and your problem is to move fast enough to get off the load of shot well ahead of the bird before it is screened within the leaves, branches, and timber.

Every now and then a new gadget comes along that is supposed to take the guesswork out of leading a moving target. All of these are just that—gadgets —and are completely useless when gunning in the field. Conceivably, such sighting devices might have some worth in shooting trap, when there is time enough to get them lined up, but, even so, I know of no expert trapshooter who resorts to gadgetry. In the first place, there is no time in field gunning to put such devices into use and, besides, shotgun shooting is not precision work. It takes artistry in movement, close coordination between hand and eye plus years of experience, to make a truly good field shot.

In the course of many years of upland shooting, you will encounter a fairly wide variety of different game species under many different shooting conditions. Throughout the country you will gun quail, woodcock, doves, grouse of several sub-species, pheasant, sage hens, and, possibly, wild turkey. You will find, too, that if you hit one species consistently you can hit them all, provided they are found in cover that will give you a chance. And hitting them, I must repeat, depends largely on your reaction time and how well you can point and fire in a hurry. One exception from the norm in this group of birds is the dove. Shooting doves is similar to pass shooting of waterfowl, which we will deal with presently.

UPLAND GAUGE, CHOKE, AND SHOT SIZE

The question of choke always enters into the problem of field shooting. Shooters are extremely selective in terms of proper choke these days, since the maximum effective pattern spread at optimum range greatly increases the probability of scoring on fast shots in tight cover.

Not too many years ago it was impossible to walk into a gun shop of average size and buy anything in a repeating shotgun except full choke, or any combination in a double gun other than modified and full. Fortunately, because of shooter awareness and demand, gun dealers now carry guns in several degrees of choke and guns fitted with variable chokes which provide the maximum selection.

Full chokes are, obviously, designed for maximum pattern density at the longest range for any given gauge. In a 12 gauge gun with an Express (or duck) load, this should be a sure killer at 60 yards; add two or three yards for a short Magnum and extend this to 70 yards for the three inch Magnum shell. It is *also* a tight shooting choke at close range, which limits the spread of pattern and therefore makes it necessary to point your gun with greater accuracy to make kills. Further, the full choke is a bad mangler of game at close range; when you do connect, you often wish you hadn't, as you pick up a grouse, or squirrel, or woodcock that is little more than a ragged mess.

Since no one attempts to kill upland game at 60 yards (or at least they shouldn't), there is no logic in using a full choke 12 gauge gun for this shooting. Over the years it has been definitely shown that kills of upland game average not more than half this distance, or 30 yards. And with some bird species, notably quail and woodcock, your kills will seldom be made at more than 20 yards. And you will get many such 20 yard shots at grouse and ringnecks when you are gunning over good pointing dogs.

Therefore the question of proper choke becomes relatively simple. For upland shooting, you buy a gun having a degree of choke that will throw an escape-proof pattern with your chosen shot size at the 30 yard range. And this is never full choke in any gauge except the little .410, which isn't really a game getting gun anyway.

In a 12 gauge gun, *cylinder bore* (no choke at all) does this nicely with the proper size and amount of shot. (We will cover shot choices in a moment.) Many users of the 12 gauge insist on some degree of choke, but it is only necessary for large birds such as pheasant, turkey, or waterfowl at long range. Otherwise, a cylinder bore will help you connect. In the 16 and 20 gauge, the *improved cylinder* does a similar job; in the 28 gauge, the *modified* choke matches this performance. But it also depends on the amount of shot you are shooting in the various gauges.

Users of the 12 gauge will find that even a cylinder bore throws a too dense pattern when the gun is firing a maximum load of 1¼ ounces of shot. Logic then suggests that there is no need for such a heavy charge of shot—about 430 pellets in a #7½ field load; some 500 in a #8 field; and approximately 730 in a #9 field. A lighter, more sensible load—dram equivalent, 1⅛ ounce standard one—delivers a clean killing, nonmangling pattern from 20 to 30 yards. In the smaller bore sizes, the 16 gauge one ounce standard load and 20 gauge one ounce "Express" load give virtually the same performance in an improved cylinder choke as the standard 12 gauge does with a cylinder bore at the same ranges—20 to 30 yards.

The man using a double gun has an advantage in this matter of choke. One barrel can be choked as we mentioned above; his second barrel can be bored improved cylinder in 12 gauge, modified in 16 or 20, and full in 28 gauge—for that occasional longer second shot, say up to 35 yards or even a bit more. When these proper degrees of choke are complemented with an effective shot size, they are deadly for all upland game shooting with the possible exception of turkey. They will give the maximum pattern spread at short range—to give you every advantage in placing the load on the target—and will also put plenty of shot into the bird up to the longest practical upland gunning ranges.

Again, we have another key phrase, "effective shot size." Too many scatter-gunners use shot that is too large. It is folly, for example, to use ⚹2 shot on ringnecks, yet many hunters do. With large shot, the pattern density becomes thin and spotty since the number of shot in the load is reduced. This gives you fewer chances of putting pellets into vital areas, which are the head, neck, and chest cavity. It is almost impossible for a good shooter to miss the head or neck area of a pheasant with a load of ⚹7½ shot in a 12 gauge gun at 35 yards, whereas it is pure luck to hit either of these vital areas with ⚹2 shot at the same range. The man who shoots ⚹2s (and, frequently, ⚹4s) is the hunter who chases many wing tipped pheasants and loses a fair percentage even with a good dog. But the smaller shot sizes really pepper the bird, usually dropping him stone dead with hits in the head and neck and at least breaking legs and wings to firmly anchor him.

Up to the limit of practical upland furred or feathered game hunting range, ⚹7½ shot will give ample penetration to create shock, which is the killing factor. A dozen pellets of this size are much deadlier than three hits with big shot (⚹2 or ⚹4), and a strong bird like a pheasant can take several big pellets in the body and keep traveling. The bird will inevitably die, but will not be recovered by the hunter.

A polished upland gunner knows when to shoot and when *not to shoot*, which means that he does not take wild chances at birds that are out of clean killing range. In close cover shooting, such as in grouse or woodcock shooting, the temptation to take a long shot is seldom offered, since a bird 35 yards away is usually out of sight. However, in hunting open cover birds, pheasants in particular, the bird is big enough to offer an appealing target as it sails out over corn stubble or marsh at 60 yards or more. No real sportsman tries such shots. The chances of inflicting wounds that may prove fatal are high; the chances of making a kill extremely low. The rule is to know the maximum killing range of your gun and load and to *stick to that range*.

WATERFOWL SHOOTING

There are added problems in waterfowl gunning. You will frequently get, in duck hunting, shots that are similar to those in the uplands, and your technique in shooting will, of course, be the same. "Jump shooting" from a poled or paddled duck boat will give you shots similar to taking ringnecks in standing corn; ducks that have dropped into your decoys and are flushed will give you shooting like that of quail or grouse—but there the similarity generally ends.

With few exceptions, and these always occur in shooting over decoys, killing a duck or a goose requires somewhat different gunning methods. For one

In "jump shooting," you move along in your boat until you get within shotgun range of the birds.

In this kind of waterfowl shooting, you wait for your shots until birds are attracted to your decoys.

thing, the ranges are invariably longer than in upland bird shooting and you have more time to get set and make your shot. Only rarely will a duck or goose speed in and pass your blind without giving you a few seconds to check his flight line and to make a guess at the range and the amount of lead you will need.

Your gun handling is basically no different from that in upland field shooting, but you will be shooting a gun more closely choked (for the added killing range you need and not, despite misconceptions, for added velocity). This means you will need to point a bit closer, but you will have more time to mount your gun and go into a steady swing.

The necessary lead in wildfowl shooting is usually so much longer than for upland game that expert upland gunners often connect with only a bird or two after firing their first box of shells at wildfowl. The explanation is simple: ducks and geese fly faster than upland birds, they fly at sharp angles

This is pass shooting, long range hunting of waterfowl, in which you try for them as they fly overhead.

to the gunner, and, invariably, are killed at longer range. All of these factors add up to a healthy length of lead.

In field shooting, the birds usually move away from the gunner. They start at a point fairly close to him, then take some slightly angling or a straight-away course, requiring a small amount of lead or none at all, depending upon the flight line. It is not often that an upland gunner gets a right angle crossing or direct incoming shot. But in wildfowling these shots are the rule rather than the exception.

A duck crossing in front of the shooter at 40 yards—which is a comfortable killing range—will usually be moving twice as fast as a grouse and will be 10 or 15 yards farther away than most grouse you will have killed. To kill a grouse under normal conditions, meaning a sharp quartering angle at about 25 yards, I, personally, will lead the bird about a length and a half. To kill the duck at 40 yards as he wings by at a right angle, I will lead him by at least six lengths. If the bird is a canvasback driven by a stiff tail wind, I will lead him 10 lengths. (Different species of ducks travel at different speeds—the diving ducks are always faster than the dipper species.)

Again, reaction time and speed of swing vary greatly in duck and goose shooting, even more than in upland gunning. For the beginner there are no rules, but one hint will help: make a guess at the amount of lead you will need, then *double it!* It is highly unlikely that anyone ever missed a duck or goose by shooting too far ahead of it. So, if you are not connecting at first, keep stepping up your lead until you do.

Once in my early days of duck shooting, when limits were 20 birds a day, I accidentally got a real clue to the problem of lead. I was gunning from a point well out in a river; fairly large flocks of mallards were passing in a flight line about 40 yards out from shore, with a big assist from a biting north wind. At first, I was picking out lone birds straying from the flocks on my side of the river, hoping for a bit closer shot, but I burned half a box of shells without disturbing a feather. Finally, a tight string of birds approached, and as they swept by I fired at the lead bird. To my great surprise—and chagrin—the *third* bird in line dropped, hitting the water with a smack! I needed to double my length of lead. By doing so, I gathered 10 mallards with the remaining shells in the box.

Since duck and goose shooting is often deliberate in both the point and the swing, some gunners adopt a different method of making the swing and follow-through from that used in the uplands—which is "swing past and pull." The alternate method, usually termed "pointing out," is to line the gun muzzle ahead of the bird at what seems to be the proper lead length, then to maintain this amount of lead until the gun is fired, following through, of course, by keeping this lead even after you pull the trigger. This is the principle of sustained lead and it works for many wildfowlers but not, I confess, for me.

THE PROBLEM OF RANGE

Since ducks and geese can be seen at very long range, the question of how far away you can kill one becomes a matter of critical judgment. With the fairly recent development of more and bigger Magnum guns and ammunition, the novice is always tempted to fire at birds well out of killing range, hoping, always hoping, that a couple or three pellets will find their mark in a vital spot. It is bad sportsmanship to fire at such birds. Kill them you might, but they will seldom die quickly enough for you to recover them. And regardless of what you may read about guns and shells that will kill at 80 yards, the gun and load have not yet been made that will *consistently* put enough shot into birds at this distance to make clean kills.

Furthermore, it is difficult enough to make accurate lead judgments in duck and goose shooting at 40 and 50 yard ranges without attempting to make such calculations at 70 yards or more. Once a shot charge passes the 50 yard mark, its velocity falls enormously but the speed of the bird remains the same. Therefore a proper lead at 50 yards will need to be trebled or quadrupled for a 70 yard hit, and the shooter who can make this kind of judgment (in addition to allowing for the drop of the shot) is rare indeed.

As a help in judging range, some wildfowlers plant a decoy about 40 yards from the blind and use it as a marker to help them estimate distances as birds pass over. Others rely upon seeing details of the plumage, in good light, as a measure of killing range. The size of the bird as it compares with your front sight bead can also be used as a range finder to some degree but *only* when you are familiar with the different species in flight and how they compare with each other in size. There is wide variation in sizes of wildfowl, from the tiny green winged teal to the big corn fed mallard or the black duck to the Canada or snow goose.

WATERFOWL GAUGE, CHOKE, AND SHOT SIZE

Unlike the wide choice that the upland gunner has, your gun should be a 12 gauge, in any style you prefer, but at first you will gain nothing by stuffing it with short Magnum loads carrying 1½ ounces of shot. Take your birds at modest ranges, not over 50 yards, and experiment with different leads until you connect. For dipper, or freshwater, ducks, #6 shot is a good choice; for diving, or sea, ducks, #4 or #5 should be used, for these ducks are larger and more heavily feathered than the dippers. If you use a gun smaller than a 12 gauge, #6 shot will do the job for all kinds of duck shooting because of the greater number of shot in each load. For geese, the minimum shot size is #4; a 12 gauge gun is the only one you should use for this sport.

The use of short Magnums or three inch Magnums will add a few yards to your effective killing range, but never in direct proportion to the percentage increase of shot in the shell. This is true for ducks, geese, and any other kind of bird shooting you do. If you do use Magnums, however, use the same shot size as you do in the Express loads we have been talking about. And as you've probably gathered, a full choke is the wildfowler's choice, regardless of shot size, because of the length of range.

In any case, if you are gunning over decoys, wait out the birds until they set their wings for a landing. This kind of easy shooting will restore your confidence if you have been running up a string of misses on passing ducks or geese.

Before leaving the subject of shot sizes for waterfowl, some comment is needed regarding recent trends and possible future developments. In some areas, lead poisoning of waterfowl has become a problem. When small, light shot pellets fall on fairly hard ground or even mud, they don't sink in quickly. Ducks sometimes ingest them while pecking for the pebbles, bits of mollusk shell, and other grit that helps their gizzards to grind their food. After some time, the lead pellets begin to dissolve or grind away, and the ducks contract lead poisoning, which is sometimes lethal. Because this happens most often with small, light shot, many game managers have come to feel that #6 should not be used. Unfortunately, however, #5 lost its popularity years ago and has become increasingly difficult to obtain. And even though the problem is serious only in certain areas, the government now plans to ban lead shot along some flyways—and ultimately lead may be banned for waterfowling everywhere.

Experiments are being conducted by game departments and ammunition manufacturers to find a satisfactory substitute for lead. Pure iron or steel is poor ballistically and tends to damage some gun barrels, but there is an excellent likelihood that a combination of iron and lead will meet all the requirements—including harmlessness when ingested by waterfowl. When such shot is introduced for general use, pellet sizes will change because the new material will be of a different weight and density than pure lead.

Chapter 8

HOW TO SHOOT BIG GAME
WITH A SHOTGUN

Although the shooting of big game is the traditional and practical province of the rifleman, such hunting sometimes has to be done with a shotgun. The rapid spread of our most popular big game animal, the whitetail deer, into farmlands and suburbs where houses and people are numerous has forced legal restrictions to be placed on the use of high powered rifles because of their lethal potential at long distances. To cut down this danger, in many states, and in individual counties within some states, only shotguns and the rifled slug (or buckshot in some cases) may legally be used in taking big game. This game is almost always whitetail deer, but black bear is also sometimes hunted with slugs—if the range is short.

This is an unfortunate situation, wasteful and occasionally inhumane. A shotgun has neither the accuracy nor the killing power of the center-fire big game rifle, so the inevitable result is a high rate of wounds to game, causing slow and painful death to the animal, but scored as a total loss to the hunter. Some of this can be traced to the use of shotguns without added rifle type sights. Such sights—iron or low power scope—*must* be added to utilize whatever accuracy can be had with the slug load. After all, you are still firing from a smoothbore gun, and even though the slug itself is grooved so that it spins somewhat like a bullet leaving a rifle barrel, it has little of a rifle bullet's accuracy.

This is not to say that, within the limit of a shotgun's effective range, a 12 gauge slug or load of buckshot isn't deadly. The big, one ounce slug has an average diameter of about .678 inch and can create a nasty wound even if it doesn't expand upon impact (and, at best, it doesn't expand a great deal).

But, let's face it, the shotgun is a short range firearm. It's doubtful if you can depend on killing big game with it any farther than you can kill ducks.

This is a 12 gauge, one ounce rifled slug; its average diameter is almost seventenths of an inch.

Again, it's not basically a matter of killing power, but at what range you can put a slug into the vital areas. I would hate to count on hitting a white-tail buck in the heart area at 75 yards with the average scope sighted smooth-bore firing the 12 gauge slug.

SIGHTS

I have tested many shotguns with slugs, ever since the first days they appeared on the market. I designed and made numerous rear sights for various guns (in the days when no such sights existed) just to see what could be done to produce deer killing accuracy. I found that, from gun to gun, you could not count on getting better accuracy than five inch groups at 50 yards from a bench rest, although some guns did better than this. I found, too, that improved cylinder and cylinder bores shot noticeably closer than full or modified chokes—due to less deformation of the slug in passage through the muzzle, I suppose. At any rate, a five inch group passes the test for hitting vital areas on a deer, and in timber hunting a great many of the shots you'll get will be at 50 yards or less. The fact is that I killed a big buck in 1948 with a 12 gauge slug, dropping him stone dead with a shot into the brisket, head on, at exactly 17 *paces*.

However, the picture has now improved considerably both with regard to

Shotguns designed especially for rifled slug shooting now have rifle type rear and front sights to increase accuracy of aiming.

guns and sights. A number of guns for slug shooting have special open bores and rifle type open rear and bead front sights. Receiver (peep) sights are also marketed. Even better, for most shooters, is a 1.5X scope like the Weaver, made just for smoothbores. It magnifies only one and a half times but you don't need enlargement at slug shooting distances. A scope clarifies the target image, and you don't have to align front and rear sights. The sight bases on Ithaca's Deerslayer autos and pumps are grooved for scope mounting, and Marlin's 55S slug gun is drilled and tapped for mount screws. Most other shotguns need a gunsmith to install a peep or scope, but a few are available from the factory with receiver sights at a slight extra cost. Many hunters find the Weaver Quik-Point even better than a scope. Somewhat resembling a high, stubby scope, it doesn't magnify but superimposes a red dot on the target. It has a side mount for gunsmith installation on most autos and pumps, and it gets on target fast enough even for shooting birds or clay targets.

If—and this is a big if—you insist upon using your upland or waterfowl gun for hunting deer with slugs, you can have problems. Number one, if you have a side by side double you will find that the two barrels do *not* shoot to the same point of impact. Some doubles spread the slugs as much as two feet at 50 yards. Next, if your bird gun is a pump or automatic, you will find that it shoots way high at the same distance. (You can counteract this by having a higher front sight installed.) And the same thing may apply if you have an over/under. The only way you can be sure about your particular

If an open rear sight isn't precise enough for you, a receiver sight like the peeps at left and above left can be installed on your slug shooting smoothbore. Even better than a peep or a scope for some shooters is the Weaver Quik-Point sight, which is fast enough for clay birding, as shown above.

This is the Ithaca Model 37 Deerslayer, a pump shotgun that is readily adaptable to the installation of a receiver sight.

gun is to test it at 40 or 50 yards, using a soft cushion for a shooting rest and squeezing off the shots just as though you were firing a rifle. In effect you *are* using a rifle of modified form, and of course you must shoot it with the deliberation you give to a rifle—not the one movement fluidity you use for a shotgun.

If you own a repeating shotgun with a variable choke device, it is well to open it up to the widest setting right away. If the choke device has inter-changeable tubes, just remove the tube entirely and shoot with the cylinder bore of the barrel. In testing guns so fitted, I have found that in some cases the slug apparently hits the edge of the choke tube if you leave one on; this results in wide shots, or "flyers." Removing the choke tube eliminates this problem.

The best course is to buy a gun just for slug shooting if a shotgun is man-datory or if you prefer one where you hunt. You will get fair groups with today's slug guns, certainly as good as five inches at 50 yards, and the chances are you will do better than this. And these guns are already equipped with open iron rifle sights that will help your cause. But it is never smart to count on hitting a deer with even these special guns at more than 75 yards. As in all shotgunning, you must know the maximum effective range of your gun and load and *stay within it*. The 12 gauge slug has power enough if you deliver it to the right spot, but you must have the right sights and type of choke to do the job.

The slug gun should certainly be zeroed in at not more than 50 yards. This means that you will hold dead on at any hunting distance up to 75 yards since there is little noticeable drop between the 50 and 75 yard range. Whatever difference there is will be lost in the wide groups you obtain at the longer range, so there is little point in worrying about it. Actual drop at 100 yards from a gun zeroed at 50 yards is only about four inches, so the slugs shoot flat enough for these timber hunting ranges.

One saving grace about shooting slugs in timber and brush is that they are real branch cutters. You can fire a slug through a mass of twigs and still count on its reaching the spot at which you aimed it. It takes a good deal to deflect one of these fat, heavy projectiles. However, they do tend to glance away from the solid objects—frozen ground, boulders, and ledges—to a much greater degree than rifle bullets, probably because of their low velocity and great mass. There is, therefore, some danger of ricochet when you use slugs.

WHERE TO AIM

As far as placing the shot is concerned, the limited accuracy of the slug load demands that you shoot for (and hit) the largest vital area. This is, of course, the chest cavity, which gives you a target on a broadside shot of about 10 by 12 inches. If your target angle is a raking one from the rear with the deer quartering away from you, your slug should be aimed to strike just behind the last rib. It will plow through the body and tear up the lungs on such a hit.

A head-on shot is more difficult since the vital area is reduced in size. I would not risk taking such a shot unless the animal were 40 yards away or less. If the deer is approaching—which is the normal assumption on head-on shots—it is smart to wait until he gets just as close as he will before he spooks. If the animal has not spotted you or caught your scent, he may come within very close range or even pass by you, giving you the easiest shot of all at the broad side of the chest cavity.

Personally, I would forego any attempt with the slug to break the deer's neck even though this is the shot I prefer to make with a rifle. I don't try for this deadly shot even with the rifle unless I *know* I can make it, and that means that the deer must be standing still and at pretty close range, say about 50 yards or less. The rifled slug doesn't give you the kind of accuracy you need to break the neck at anything like this range unless you're lucky.

It is absolutely essential that you shoot your deer hunting shotgun enough to become intimately familiar with the way it groups and its point of impact—which you can adjust if you have movable sights. Because of the fairly high cost of the slug loads, too many hunters will "try out" their guns by firing three or four slugs, then shrug and say, "Good enough." If you buy a box of slugs (25), it will pay off to shoot 20 of them on the target range and save five for your hunt. Many deer hunters reverse this count, which is poor economy since no one can be sure of what his gun is doing after firing only five shots. It only takes one to kill the deer, but you must know that you can place the slug with that one shot. Only shooting the gun can tell you this.

The best choice in gauge is, as I mentioned, the 12, shooting the one ounce slug. The 16 gauge and 20 gauge will also do the job but their slugs are proportionately smaller in diameter, making a smaller wound channel, and they have less striking energy—also in the same diminishing proportion, because the slugs are lighter in weight—⅞ ounce for the 16, ⅝ ounce for the 20. The puny 86 grain slug of the .410 is not to be considered and should be outlawed for *any* big game hunting—as it is in some states.

BUCKSHOT LOADS

The hunter who is forced to use buckshot for deer or bear (in the state of New Jersey, for example) is even less fortunate that the slug shooter. True, a load of buckshot increases the chances of hitting the target, but the power of the individual pellets is so low that the ratio of hits to kills is much less than even in slug shooting. The trouble is that the dispersion of standard buckshot is wide and uneven.

You will often hear wild tales about killing a deer at 100 yards with buckshot. These are sheer lies, poor judgment of range, or one in a million instances of outright luck in having one pellet strike the deer in the head. Your chances of killing a deer at 100 yards with buckshot are about as good as killing a grouse on the wing with a BB gun. It just doesn't happen.

Buckshot has been around for a long time, long before we had slug loads for shotguns. And since the beginning, it has performed erratically except at extremely short range. Admittedly, there is no deadlier killer than a husky load of buckshot, close up, but it must be just that—close up.

Late in 1963, Winchester introduced a new buckshot load, with the pellets enclosed in a plastic sleeve and cushioned by powdered polyethylene. There are other brands now using the same approach, but if you shoot the old, uncushioned type of buckshot load you can't count on pattern uniformity or consistency of hits beyond about 40 yards at most. Whatever brand you use, be sure they're the modern, effective, plastic wrapped and cushioned type.

Buckshot pellets, when packed in the shell, are spherical. Only if they retain this roundness in flight can they produce fairly good patterns. Unless collared and cushioned, each pellet suffers severe damage after the shell is fired: first, in the forcing cone of the barrel—the taper forward of the chamber that reduces the chamber diameter to that of the bore; next, in contact with the bore; last, as it passes through the choke. Yet in spite of all this bore deformation, the most significant factor is that of the shot being pushed together by the force of the powder gas pressure, which flattens them into weird shapes. Here is where the cushioning of powdered plastic is so important. If you have ever recovered uncushioned buckshot fired into a tank of water or some soft material such as cotton waste (both of which allow you to recover the shot in the same shape as that in which pellets reach a target) you will be amazed at the deformity. Some look like cubes, others like pyramids. None are really spherical since they have been battered around too much. Naturally, none of these deformed shot can be expected to "fly right."

RANGE AND CHOKE

Using ⚡oo Buck size (about .33 caliber, 12 pellets to a short Magnum 12 gauge shell, nine to a 12 gauge field load) or ⚡o Buck (about .30 caliber, 12 pellets to a 12 gauge field load), the safe maximum range to fire at a deer is 40 yards or so with the old-fashioned, uncushioned buckshot. At this range you *should* put four or five pellets into the body cavity and *should* find the deer dead nearby without much trailing involved. If you try to stretch the range by taking shots at more than 50 yards, you may wound several deer before you drop one. With the modern collared and cushioned buckshot loads, you get the same number of pellets, and the maximum range is closer to 60 yards.

Uncushioned buckshot performs best in guns with little or no choke. Since most guns do have some choke, it's important to pattern your gun and decide on the limit of its killing pattern, then respect this maximum range when hunting deer. The collared and cushioned buckshot performs best with a full choke and can therefore be used to good advantage in a tightly choked gun such as you might also use for some of your waterfowling. But as with slugs, it's wise to install rifle sights for buckshot hunting.

THE PLASTIC SHOT COLLAR AND CUSHION

The last decade's development of plastic not only for the shell walls but inside buckshot loads merits a bit more descriptive detail here, because it is the *only* significant improvement in buckshot shells in almost a century. First a polyethylene sleeve was wrapped around the shot charge; then the space between the individual pellets was packed with powdered polyethylene. This shields the pellets from a large portion of bore contact—in the forcing cone, barrel interior, and choke. At the same time, the cushioning effect of the powdered plastic effectively reduces the jamming of the pellets against one another, so far less deformation is produced as the pellets are hurled forward by powder gas pressure.

Buckshot now produces much more uniform patterns at all ranges, and the spread has been tightened up by as much as 50 percent in some guns. In the hunter's terms, it means the chance to make a clean kill with ⚔oo or ⚔o

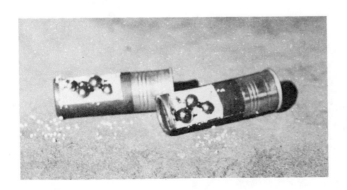

Here, with their sides cut away, are a couple of buckshot loads that utilize a polyethylene sleeve around the shot charge and the same plastic in powdered form to pack the space between pellets.

buckshot at 50 yards or even slightly more has been almost doubled. In fact, I have a 12 gauge three inch Magnum pump gun, full choke, which, when loaded with a modern three inch shell carrying 15 #00 Buck pellets, puts eight or nine shot into the body area of a deer outline target with great consistency at 50 yards. For the buckshot shooter, this means that his scattergun is now a reasonably good deer killer and he can use his full choke pump gun in the knowledge that he is carrying the most effective firearm he can use with buckshot.

Nonetheless, buckshot remains a load of limited range and it is nothing less than sinful to try for deer at 75 yards or more, no matter what the circumstances. Again, shoot that gun—a bit more deliberately than you would a bird gun—learn what it will do, and stay within that killing range.

Chapter 9

HOW TO SHOOT HANDGUNS

Contrary to the myth of the Old West popularized by movies and television, most sidearms are useful with iron sights only within a limit of about 50 yards. To be sure, the .44, .41 and .357 Magnums and a few varmint handgun cartridges shoot accurately (though less so than a rifle) at greater distances, but only in the hands of an expert. For the beginner, practice at 50 feet produces the best results; at greater distances the target is simply too difficult to hit. And the learning arm should be a .22.

If you're like most shooters, you won't be satisfied with mediocre marksmanship, but in order to become really good you must learn what a handgun can do, then practice doing it . . . and then practice some more. The first thing to learn is how the gun operates.

There are three common types of handgun: the single action revolver, the double action revolver, and the autoloading, so-called automatic, pistol. A fourth basic type, for specialized use, is the single shot. In International match shooting, for the "free pistol" events, a .22 rim-fire falling block design such as the Hammerli is representative. Another free pistol, developed by Olympic shooter Franklin Green, employs a bolt action with an electrically operated trigger mechanism. For informal shooting, chiefly varmint hunting, two popular center-fire single shots are the bolt action Remington XP-100, chambered for the .221 Remington Fireball cartridge, and the Thompson/Center Contender, a break open pistol available with interchangeable barrels in a number of calibers.

In terms of all-around reliability, the revolvers have a slight edge on the automatic; they have less tendency to malfunction because of a faulty magazine or dirty action. Moreover, revolvers in .22 caliber, .357 Magnum, .41 Magnum, and .44 Magnum give you a choice of different loads. For example, most .22 rim-fires handle Short, Long, or Long Rifle ammo; .357 Magnums take the Magnum load and the wide variety of .38 Special cartridges; the .41 Magnum uses either a standard or heavy load; the .44 Magnum takes the Magnum load, the .44 Special, and the .44 Russian.

Since a consistent blowback pressure must be maintained for the self-loading feature of any type or caliber of automatic pistol to function, only the specific cartridge for which the gun is designed will operate it properly (except for single shot use).

THE SINGLE ACTION REVOLVER

Today's single action handguns are either duplicates of the famous old "six-gun" of the West or improved mechanical designs of the same basic type. You'll find when you hold one that this is a good shape—comfortable in your hand.

Both single and double action revolvers operate on the same principle. The cylinder is revolved by a small metal projection called the hand, which is attached to the hammer and projects through the recoil plate to engage ratchet notches on the rear of the cylinder. Each time you cock your gun, the cylinder turns one notch.

The firing principle is also similar for both types of revolver. The trigger sear rests in a notch of the hammer sear. Pulling the trigger disengages these

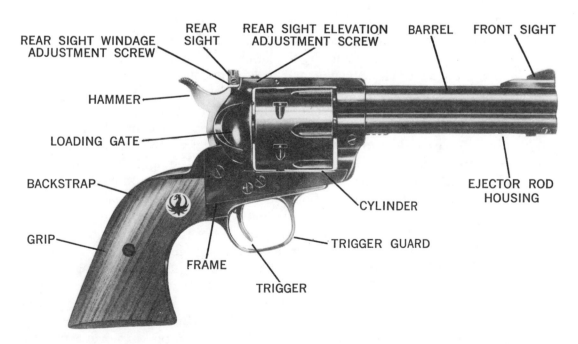

Here is a typical modern single action revolver; the parts that you should be familiar with are pointed out.

To fire a single action, you must pull the hammer back to its rearmost station and then pull the trigger.

sears and the hammer falls, under pressure from the gun's mainspring. When the hammer is at full cock, a cylinder lock engages a notch to keep the chamber aligned with the bore.

So much for the similarities between single and double actions; now for the differences. Most important, of course, is that the former can only be fired by cocking the hammer manually and then pulling the trigger, whereas trigger pull alone will cock and fire the latter. The single action is undoubtedly the strongest of all handguns and will stand long, hard use without malfunction. The frame is a one piece drop forging, with no cuts for cylinder swing-out to weaken its over-all strength. It has fewer moving (and delicate) parts than double action models and is less temperamental in general. It is, however, slow to reload because you must feed the cartridges into the chambers one at a time through a loading gate on the right side of the frame. You must also punch out the fired cases one at a time through this gate.

Characteristically, single action guns have a long hammer fall and a fairly heavy hammer. If, like many marksmen, you want the best target performance, you may prefer the shorter, snappier fall of the double action hammer; this shortens lock time—the interval between the release of the trigger and the ignition of the cartridge. Some slight movement of the gun can always be expected during this time, and it may affect the alignment of your sights as the shot gets away. Lock time, and the moment in which your sights can go off target, is shorter with a double action. Moreover, it is not as easy, mechanically, to produce a clean, sharp, light trigger pull in single action design as in double action. The latter is therefore the choice of many accuracy conscious shooters.

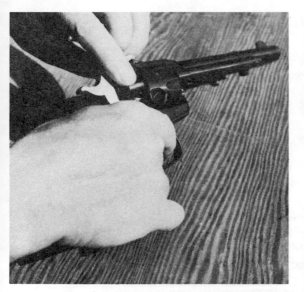 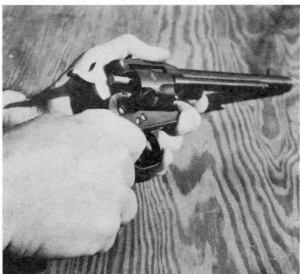

Loading and unloading a single action is a comparatively slow process. To load, you must place a cartridge in a chamber, revolve the cylinder, and insert the next shell, and so on until the gun is fully loaded. Unloading is similar in that you must eject one cartridge at a time, turning the cylinder to align each chamber with the ejector and the loading gate.

Because you must always be aware of the safety features of your gun, it's a good idea to practice with them until their operation becomes second nature. If you're using a single action, thumb the hammer back slowly; when it has moved about one-eighth inch it will click. That means you've engaged the safety notch. This safety station, or half-cock as it is called, is the *only* safety on a single action, so learn to use it. When you move the hammer back another one-fourth inch it will be at the loading station and you can spin the cylinder to align its chambers with the loading gate; practice that, too. Now move the hammer all the way back and your gun is at full cock, ready to fire.

A great deal of hunting, plinking, and target shooting is done with .22 caliber handguns, but this isn't the only reason to stick with the .22 as a learning and practice arm—regardless of whether you pick a single action, a double action, or an auto. You can buy a .22 at a modest price, and ammunition for it costs less than that for the higher calibers (unless you reload your own, in which case you *must* have a center-fire model because rim-fires can't be hand loaded). Aside from the matter of expense, you'll do well with a .22 because it's accurate, comparatively quiet, and has virtually no recoil.

THE DOUBLE ACTION REVOLVER

The term double action refers to a mechanical system that allows this handgun design to be fired in two ways: first, you can simply pull the trigger, thereby cocking the hammer, revolving the cylinder to bring a cartridge into alignment with the bore and hammer, and, in the same cycle of

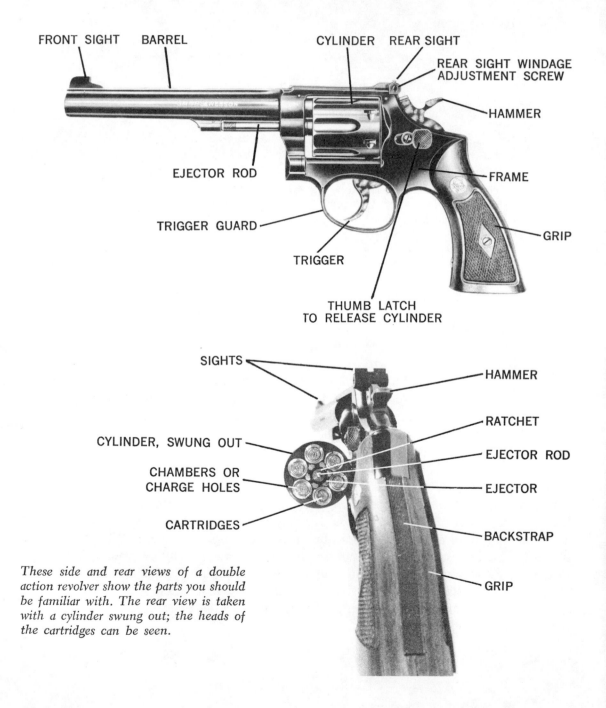

These side and rear views of a double action revolver show the parts you should be familiar with. The rear view is taken with a cylinder swung out; the heads of the cartridges can be seen.

A double action revolver can be fired in one of two ways: simply by pulling the trigger, as in the first photo, or by manually cocking the gun and then pulling the trigger—the same way a single action must be fired—as in the second picture.

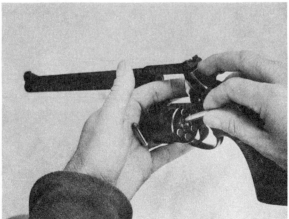

Here is a double action revolver with its cylinder swung to the side, ready for loading, with cartridges being inserted into the cylinder. Not only is loading faster than with a single action, but one push of the ejector rod, shown at the front of the cylinder in the first picture, kicks out all the empties. The one-at-a-time extraction that is part of single action guns is not the case here.

movement, firing the gun; second (the method commonly used), you can thumb the hammer back to the full cock notch—which rotates the cylinder— and then pull the trigger.

The latter method actually amounts to firing a double action like a single action; when you manually cock the gun, you bring the trigger back to a position where you can reach it more easily with the tip of your forefinger, and you can fire the arm by applying a relatively light trigger pressure. It is only when fired this way that double actions have a sharp, short, target quality trigger pull. Such a revolver is only used as a double action (without first cocking it) in situations of extreme urgency or by specialists for timed and rapid fire target shooting.

Double action guns have the advantage of fast, easy loading and unloading: hold the gun in your right hand, swing the cylinder out (to the left) and, when it's in this position, eject the fired cases simultaneously with a push of the ejector rod. You can then reload it quickly.

Double actions have a safety *block* rather than a safety notch. This block is internal—not controlled by the shooter—and it keeps the hammer from striking until you cock it manually or exert a long, strong trigger pull to cock and fire. With the hammer forward (uncocked) the gun can't go off accidentally even if it is dropped or the hammer struck a sharp blow. For this reason, the double action is extremely safe.

When you pull the hammer all the way back, the gun is cocked; this motion should also be practiced. In Chapter 2 we advised dry firing a rifle to get the feel of the arm. You should become familiar with your handgun in the same way.

THE AUTOMATIC PISTOL

The most outstanding (but often overrated) feature of the automatic is speed of fire for repeat shots. In rapid fire target work this assumes great importance, hence the popularity of the auto for competition in all match calibers—.22, .38, and .45. The .22 rim-fire autos have always been tops for paper target shooting; more recently factory made .38s, in addition to the custom versions and the "accurized" .45s, have dominated the center-fire matches.

In hunting, however, the auto's speed is far less important, since a handgunner generally takes his time when trying for game and doesn't restrict himself to standardized shooting form. As a rule, the first accurately placed bullet does the job, so you'll want to make every effort to get off that single, carefully held, deliberately squeezed off shot, using the steadiest position you can develop. This means that form won't matter much to you; you'll be shooting from a prone or sitting position as often as standing. You'll em-

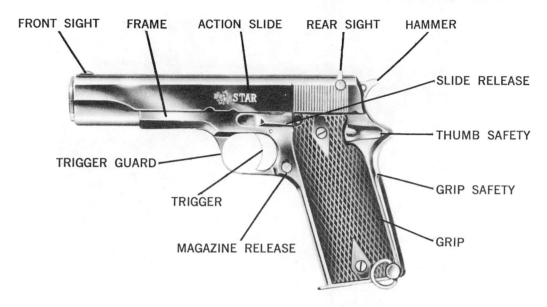

FRONT SIGHT   FRAME   ACTION SLIDE   REAR SIGHT   HAMMER

SLIDE RELEASE

STAR

THUMB SAFETY

TRIGGER GUARD

GRIP SAFETY

TRIGGER

GRIP

MAGAZINE RELEASE

The labels show the important parts of an autoloading pistol.

ploy a rest if possible, or use your knees for support in the sitting position. And even with a rest, hold your gun with both hands.

We advised you to handle and dry fire the revolver. This is just as important with an automatic, and if you can get hold of a couple of different models to examine before buying one, you'll be still better off because there is greater variation in automatic design than in that of the revolver. You must pull back the slide to chamber the first cartridge in almost all autos; on subsequent shots it operates on blowback pressure, which pushes the breechblock back to eject the spent shell. As the block comes forward again, it picks up the top cartridge in the spring clip, which is located in the grip, and chambers a round as it returns to position. In some models, the receiver slides back with the breechblock.

Safety devices differ on the various automatics. They all have a thumb operated safety at the side, but many have one or even two additional safety systems. Some (primarily the hammerless "pocket" autos) have an additional grip safety which must be depressed in order to fire; some won't fire if you take out the magazine clip; some hammer autos have a safety notch much like that on a revolver. There are models with one or a combination of safeties; become thoroughly familiar with your gun.

Multiple safeties on some models may lead you to believe that the automatic is the safest type of side arm. This is not true. If you're going to carry a gun loaded and ready to fire, a revolver is safer than a single action auto-

Just as with autoloading shoulder arms, you must manually activate an automatic pistol for its first shot. With a handgun, you have to pull back the slide; this cocks the gun and chambers a cartridge.

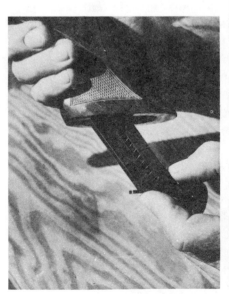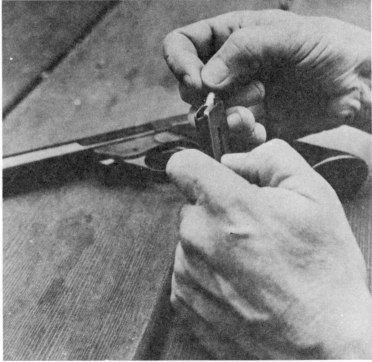

Ammunition for autos is stored in a clip, usually in the gun's grip. You load cartridges into this clip just as you do into the clip of a rifle.

All autos have a thumb safety; some have additional devices such as the grip safety that is indicated on the small, hammerless pistol. The latter device must be depressed in order for the gun to fire.

GRIP
SAFETY

matic. (A single action auto is one that requires cocking for the first shot; a double action doesn't, but only a few double action autos are made.) To fire a revolver, you must cock the hammer manually and then fire (single action), or exert a long, strong pull to cock it and fire (double action). A live cartridge need not be under the hammer, because cocking rotates the cylinder to position the shell you're going to fire. A ready to fire auto, however, not only has a live shell in the chamber, but the hammer is half-cocked—or on full cock with the safety on—even though the gun may still be in its holster. Because the hammer is concealed in the so-called hammerless automatic (which utilizes an internal hammer), it's easier to fire such a model accidently. Bear this in mind when choosing a gun.

THE HANDGUN GRIP

Accurate shooting begins with your grip. When you have a firm hold on your gun, you can keep the sights aligned, control the effects of recoil, and, with a revolver, place your thumb in the proper position to cock the hammer for successive shots.

It is important not only to develop the correct grip but to *maintain* it with rigid uniformity. If your hold changes from shot to shot or from day to day, you'll never shoot tight groups consistently or even be able to tell how accurately your gun is firing. The recoil of the gun in your hand vitally affects it from shot to shot. That is why you should start with a .22; it has minimal recoil. But when you graduate to, say, a .44 Magnum, recoil will be a big factor; your grip should be perfected before you use such a big bore.

It's easy with an automatic; there is only one way to grip it—the natural way, just as you would a saw handle. But with a revolver, beginners usually make the mistake of gripping it like a fishing rod or a golf club. Instead, shift your hand around the grip so that the fleshy pad at the base of the thumb aids in holding. The thumb must be level or high up on the side of the frame

These side and rear views show the proper way to grip an autoloading pistol.

and far enough forward to touch the recoil plate behind the cylinder. Naturally, the size of your hand will determine its exact position, but the important thing is to make sure the backstrap is supported by the meatiest part of the base of your thumb.

This "rule of thumb" can be varied to insure your being able to cock the hammer easily; this can be accomplished by shifting your hand higher up on the grip without changing the center-line relationship. Try it and you'll see that the higher you can hold the gun without interfering with the hammer at full cock, the better your grip will be. Ideally, with the ball of your forefinger on the trigger, your remaining fingers should be firmly positioned around the grip, though with a large hand and a small revolver this is not always possible.

To hold the gun steady, exert pressure between the front of the grip and the backstrap—*not on the sides*. Try to maintain this pressure without interfering with the action of your trigger finger; this may feel awkward at first,

These top and side views illustrate the proper way to grip a revolver, utilizing the meatiest part of the hand, at the base of the thumb, to support the gun at the backstrap.

but the direct fore and aft pressure keeps shots in line vertically, whereas side pressure shifts the bullet impact to the right or left.

It takes long practice to hold your gun firmly with the thumb and three fingers without influencing, or being influenced by, the trigger finger. It's something like the trick of rubbing your stomach in a rotary motion with one hand while patting the top of your head with the other. In handgun shooting, grip and trigger squeeze must be independent of each other. Even when you shoot with a rest, after the first few times only your *hand* is steadied; the gun doesn't touch the rest, so steadiness depends on your grip. To squeeze the trigger, draw your finger straight back without squeezing the *gun*.

ANALYZING ERRORS ON THE TARGET

The position of the shooting hand, the trigger finger, and various pressures on the gun, as well as trouble caused by anticipating the shot, can produce some predictable results in the placement of the bullet. Ignition time, or lock time, also can be a disturbing factor if your shooting hand is not performing as it should. Some groups of shots not centered in the bull tell their own story if you can read cause and effect.

If, for example, your handgun is properly sighted-in and suddenly you discover that you are grouping your shots a bit low and to the left (about eight o'clock), it is likely that you are placing your trigger finger too far into the trigger guard and pressing off the shot with an angular rather than a straight back movement. Then, when the sear releases the hammer, this angular movement follows through during the time of the hammer fall, shifting the gun slightly to the left and low just before the cartridge fires. A group that strikes on the opposite side of the target (about four o'clock) is the result of tightening the grip of the entire hand as the trigger is squeezed off, shifting the gun to the right and low.

"Thumbing" the frame on the left side by increasing thumb pressure as the gun fires usually gives groups on the right side (three o'clock position), since just enough side pressure occurs to shift the arm to the right as the hammer falls. A group striking well below the bull (six o'clock position) suggests that the recoil is being anticipated and you are "breaking" your wrist, which drops the gun slightly as the hammer falls.

One insidious aspect of these off-center problems is that they are difficult to detect since they take place *after* you have released the trigger. Hence, the importance of an extremely smooth trigger squeeze and a constant, unchanging grip until the gun actually fires. This is the reverse of following through on your swing with a shotgun; no added movement should be involved in holding and gripping the gun until the shot gets away.

SIGHT ALIGNMENT

When your grip, pressure, and sight alignment are all correct, you'll begin to get bull's-eyes. The importance of the sight picture can't be overemphasized. Carelessness in *precise* alignment—not only the relationship of front to rear sight but of both to the target—is the downfall of the average beginner.

The short sighting radius—i.e., the distance between front and rear sights—multiplies sighting errors four or five times compared to similar errors made with a rifle. In addition to the sights being closer to each other, a handgun's rear sight is farther from your eye than a rifle's, and this adds to the difficulty of lining up the sights. Oddly enough, you must not try to shorten this distance; to maintain a steady hold and horizontal alignment, you must point the gun straight out, with the sights as far from your eye as possible.

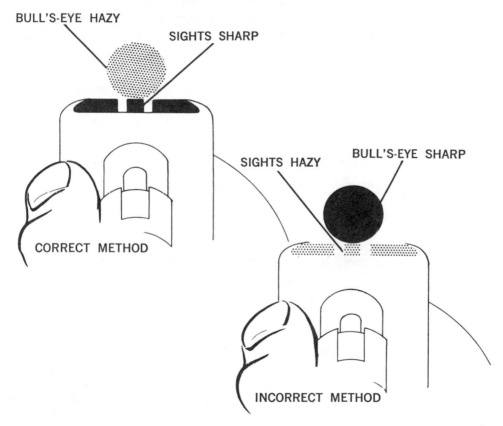

When you first sight down a handgun at a target, you'll notice that you can't focus on rear sight, front sight, and target at the same time. You can focus on the target, leaving your sights blurred, or you can keep the sights in focus and let the target blur. This latter method is correct, because if the sights are not sharp, you can't aim properly.

Place the front sight exactly in the middle of the rear sight notch, with an equal "line of white" (the amount of target showing) on either side of the front sight. Make certain the top of the front sight is exactly even with the top of the rear sight's sides and see that both sights are vertical.

You'll notice that you can't get clear definition of the sights and the target at the same time. This is because no normal eye can focus simultaneously on two objects that are a considerable distance apart. If your focus on the sights is sharp, the target is slightly blurred; if you focus on the target, your sights will be indistinct. You must make a choice, and the top marksmen choose a clear view of the sights. Keep both eyes open, focus on the sights, and you'll find that you can hit the target, blurred though it is. To be exact, focus just on the *front* sight. The rear sight will be only slightly blurred; alignment will be sharp enough for accurate shooting.

In rifle shooting with open sights, a crack shot usually shifts his point of focus several times between sights and target before firing, even though he may not be aware of it. But in handgun sighting there is no firm support to keep the sights in line while the shooter does this shifting. The best method is to bring your sights to bear on the target quickly, then focus on the sights until you've touched off your shot. Doing this—especially with both eyes open —won't be easy at first, but it will bring about an improvement in accuracy that will be well worth the long hours of practice.

THE AIMING AREA

In target shooting, a handgun is sighted to place the bullets in the center of the bull's-eye using a six o'clock hold—i.e., with your front sight barely touching the center bottom of the bull. This will keep the black circle of the target entirely visible and prevent the black of the sights from blending into the black of the bull. The six o'clock hold is less satisfactory for field and small game shooting, however, since this demands that you sight in the gun to shoot higher than the actual aiming area. The advantage of having an adjustable rear sight on a handgun is that you can raise or lower it to suit the occasion and move it right or left for windage. For target shooting, the six o'clock hold is great. If you're hunting or plinking, you can adjust the rear sight so that the area you'll hit is exactly the one you're aiming at.

We say *area* rather than *point* of aim because it's hard to be more precise with only the sights in sharp focus. The exception is when you have a solid rest and time to adjust your sight picture more critically by shifting your focus to the target briefly, then back to the sights.

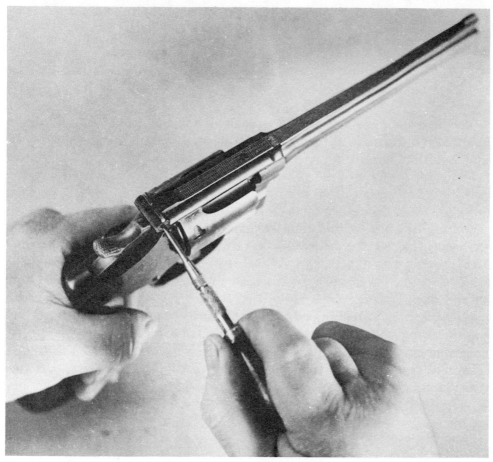

Adjustable sights on a pistol can be changed simply by turning a couple of screws. The first picture shows a windage adjustment being made; the second photo shows elevation being corrected.

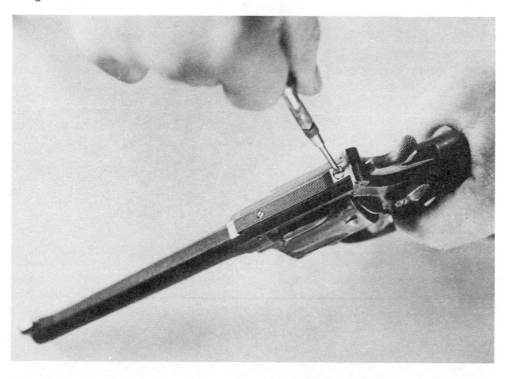

FIRING THE SHOT

The final and most important step in accurate handgun shooting is trigger squeeze. No matter how well you grip the gun and align the sights, your shot won't center on the target if you don't touch off the trigger perfectly.

Fire your handgun like a rifle, gradually increasing your finger pressure until the hammer falls. Pull the trigger by placing the pad, or ball, of your index finger on the center of the trigger in such a position that movement (and pressure) *straight back* fires the gun. Proper coordination between hand and eye is vital, for the sights must be kept in alignment with each other and with the target as the pressure is increased. No one can hold a gun absolutely steady; the sights weave around the target, from side to side and up and down, as pressure is applied to the trigger. But once this pressure is begun, it must be continued until the gun fires—or you must bring your gun down and start all over again. If you relax trigger pressure but try to keep your grip and sight picture, you are likely to "freeze" on the trigger again and again until you suddenly jerk the shot off. In the event that you waver completely *off* target, you must relax and start all over again.

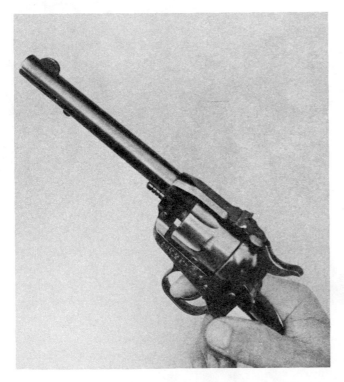

A handgun's trigger should be squeezed, just like a rifle's, with the tip of your finger utilized to apply gradually increasing pressure straight back until the shot goes off.

SHOOTING POSITIONS

If you're a beginner, there's little point in trying to assume the traditional stance of the target shooter during your first lessons in handgun shooting. Instead, steady your gun arm and, at the very beginning, the gun barrel,
with soft supports on a shooting bench or table. Only in this way can you
learn proper sight alignment, grip, and trigger squeeze. And since hunters
and field shooters are not restricted to any one position, the novice will do
well to shoot from the prone and sitting positions, using both hands to hold
the gun. We will go into more detail about these shooting positions in

*A beginning handgun shooter should take his first shots from a bench rest. In addition,
until he starts to see some results, he should rest the barrel of his gun on a soft support,
and he may even use two hands to further steady his hold. Then, before he leaves the
bench to assume more traditional and more difficult shooting stances, he should fire
from the rest with support only for his shooting hand.*

Even after leaving the bench rest, the shooter should use both hands to help him steady the gun before he goes to one hand positions.

This is the traditional arm extended method of shooting a handgun, a necessary position for target shooters to master, but one that should be approached only after the shooter has attained a degree of proficiency and confidence.

Chapter 11, "How to Shoot in the Field"; these are the ones you should use when you leave the steadiness of the shooting rest.

The offhand, arm extended, method of handgun shooting is really for the experts. It is a position every handgunner should master eventually, but it is the last step. When the time does come, most shooters are able to adapt themselves to it with little trouble—because by that time they have mastered the fundamentals. There are two schools of handgunners—those who stand at about a 90 degree angle to the target and those who prefer 45 degrees or even a little less. When you're ready to learn this position, try various angles to see which works best for you, but in doing so remember that the farther away the sights are from your eyes, the better your stance—and your accuracy—will be.

Place your feet comfortably—about 14 inches apart is usually enough, but there's no rule—turn your face to the target and put your non-shooting hand in your pocket or hook your thumb in your belt. The idea is to forget that hand and arm. The old "classic" stance with hand on hip takes effort and therefore detracts from concentration.

Now raise your gun to the target. Some shooters first point their gun straight up, but in general this is bad practice—mere theatrics—and has even led to accidental discharges in cases where trigger pull was very light. If your arm and gun are pointing straight out, you should hit at least somewhere on the target. Because the main obstacle to good shooting, as we have said, is gun waver, you *must be sure to lock your elbow.* Your entire arm and hand, except for the trigger finger, form a solid projection to assure the stability of hold and stance that results in hits.

Here are two popular single shot hunting pistols. The bolt action is the .221 Remington XP-100, a fine varminting gun. The other pistol is the Thompson/Center Contender, which accepts interchangeable barrels in many calibers and is sometimes used for larger game than varmints.

Chapter 10

HOW TO SHOOT
TARGET HANDGUNS

Match shooting with the handgun is a far different game from informal plinking, or hunting small or big game or varmints with a pistol. When you're on the target range, you must stick to the rules—and they are fairly rigid—as well as be subject to the pressure of competition and the continual noise of firing from either side. If you get a case of "buck fever," you must settle it for yourself—standing there on your two hind legs with nothing but your own nerve and self-control to pull you out.

Nevertheless, pistol shooting under match rules is one of the fastest growing shooting games in the country. For one thing, it requires a minimum of equipment—a good target gun or two, maybe three if you're going all the way, a spotting scope, and a simple box to carry all your gear. You need no special clothing, you are not encumbered with many changes of sights and scopes, and, usually, you will find pistol ranges, either indoors or outdoors, in communities where there is little or no room for rifle and shotgun shooting. It's a simpler, cozier game than other types of formal target shooting and has a heavy following during the indoor winter season.

We have already covered the basic tenets of handgun shooting in Chapter 9: method of sighting, holding the gun, trigger control, and the standing position. This is unchanged in match shooting. The difference is that added refinements—your gun, match shooting technique, off-range practice, and shooter psychology—must be dealt with.

Since a pistol shooter is essentially a one hand man, great emphasis must be placed on developing that hand and arm at the outset. A serious shooter will begin, after his first few days of experimenting on the range, to develop the muscles of his shooting arm and to perfect his trigger squeeze. Dry firing practice is the routine, coupled with added weight on the shooting arm—but more on these subjects in a moment.

The first problem of the match shooter is the gun. No better start can be had than with a .22 automatic pistol; and get a model designed for target shooting. Such guns have finely adjustable sights—extremely important—a comfortable grip that allows no mistakes in holding—a common occurrence when a tyro shoots a revolver—a good, crisp trigger pull, and superb accuracy.

From this point forward—after acquiring the handgun—you are faced with endless practice if you want to become a real competitor. And if you like to shoot, this is all to the good. At first, you'll wobble all over the target; then, as practice steadies your hand, you'll just be wobbling around the sighting black, or bull, in range terms.

What happens from then on is up to you. Of course, as we said before, your view of the sights must be clear, but it is not essential that you have the eyes of an eagle. If you wear shooting glasses (or regular glasses) you can sharpen your view of both sights and target by attaching an aperture of one kind or another to your glasses. It can be done by punching a one-

Formal target shooting with pistols is popular because, without requiring elaborate equipment, it provides the enjoyment of shooting and the thrill of competition. In this photo, members of an Army pistol team use the stance favored by today's marksmen, with the non-shooting hand tucked comfortably in the pocket.

You can fire all regulation target handguns and all regulation target events on indoor ranges.

eighth inch (or smaller) hole in a piece of masking tape and sticking this to your right (or master) eye lens wherever you look through that lens to the sights, usually about one-fourth inch from the top edge. Or you can use a piece of aluminum foil, sheet brass, or some other metal for a more permanent fix. You will need to experiment with the size of the hole since eyes vary, but you will find that this little attachment *does* sharpen up both sights and target.

It must again be stressed that *precise* alignment of the sights, as outlined in Chapter 9, is vital to good shooting. The smallest misalignment of the front and rear sights becomes a wide miss by the time the bullet hits paper, so your concentration in getting, and keeping, these sights in correct position is *far more important* than getting a dead center hold under the bull as you squeeze off.

The act of triggering off the shot is a *straight back* pressure that increases gently until the hammer falls. Correctly done, you will not really be dead sure just when the gun will fire, although, obviously, you will be holding on the bull's-eye at six o'clock as you increase this pressure.

MUSCLE CONTROL AND DRY FIRING PRACTICE

Your development program will begin with toughening up the muscles of your shooting arm. There are several ways to do this. Some shooters hang a three pound weight on the wrist, then pick up the gun and hold it in shooting position for about 30 seconds, then relax for a spell and do it again, and again, for a period of 15 minutes a day, *every* day. Another trick is to hold a heavy jack plane, which has a grip similar to that of the handgun, for this muscle strengthening practice. You should have some sort of target for an aiming point during these practice sessions, although it need not be a regulation bull—just a clearly defined aiming point. When you can hold about a three pound weight pretty steadily on the aiming point for about 30 seconds you will find that holding the gun on the bull becomes comparatively easy.

Although actual shooting is the most pleasant way to practice, it can be expensive and inconvenient to do, most of the time. You can develop good holding, good sight picture, and correct trigger control at home simply by dry firing practice *daily*. Select a target (something about the size of a 25 yard rifle target) and pin it to the wall or stick it on a window at about your eye level. Use this for developing your precise sight picture as well as for dry firing.

Usually it does no harm to dry fire a target type automatic pistol. Yet to play safe and save the firing pin, it is a good idea to do your snapping on a fired cartridge case. In a .22, you can shift this around in the chamber from time to time and get a lot of mileage out of just one case. For center-fire use, I make up dummies by turning hard fiber rod to a tight fit in the primer pocket, then pushing this plug in with the primer seater on a hand loading tool. This, naturally, doesn't work with rim-fires. If you can find dummy cartridges, that's good, but they are hard to come by in the United States in any caliber.

PRACTICING WITH LIVE AMMUNITION

At this point you will be doing all of your record shooting at slow fire with a .22—which, under match rules, gives you 10 minutes for a string of 10 shots. Once you begin to keep all your shots in the black, it is time to pay some attention to your timing, always remembering that in a match you get no added points for finishing ahead of time. Actually, there is no big hurry to get off each shot, for an average of one minute is ample time to make three or four attempts, if necessary, at a new hold. If your first hold doesn't get you on the bull when your trigger control and breathing are just right, lower the gun, take a few slow, deep breaths and try again.

If you have just gotten off a bad shot, out of the black, this may give you some momentary jitters, but don't let it trouble you too much. It can't be erased or brought back. Apply a bit more concentration on the next shot.

In any case, it is smart to take as much time as the rules allow. And, in practice, it is a good idea to lay a watch on the shooting bench so you know just how much time you are taking for each shot and how much you have left. You will soon develop a sixth sense about this and be able to estimate the one minute intervals with surprising accuracy. A stop watch is obviously a better timer than a regular watch since you won't have to trust to your memory or make a note of your starting time.

In outdoor shooting, you will find that on those days when a gusty wind is blowing you will want to take full advantage of the maximum time, so that you will be better able to get off shots when the wind subsides. This often means waiting out the wind for a minute or more, but this trick will give you more 10s than 8s.

Once you have begun to run scores in the 90s (out of 100) at slow fire, you will be anxious to begin work on timed and rapid fire. In the timed fire event you must get off two five shot strings, 20 seconds for each. Then comes rapid fire, which is two five shot strings at 10 seconds per string. For these events in the .22 class, which is what we are talking about now, it is proper to load only five cartridges into your gun, even though it will hold more—as many as 10 in an automatic. With five loaded, there is no need for you to lessen your concentration on accuracy by having to count—and no danger of disqualifying yourself by pegging a sixth shot into the target. In the center-fire events, regardless of how many cartridges your gun will hold, you only load five. (No center-fire will hold 10, and loading to full capacity of, say, six or seven, is no advantage in these target shooting events. As a matter of fact, according to one of the rules in modern matches, you're *required* to load only five cartridges.)

You can best begin practice for the timed and rapid fire events while practicing slow fire. At the beginning it will simply mean that you fire a couple of shots without lowering your arm. Then you increase to three shots at a time, and continue upward to five. Gradually you speed up your shooting, lessening the time between shots, but only if you are still getting a clear sight picture and smooth trigger control. If you find that a three shot string is too much and you are not getting into the bull, drop back to two shots. The important thing is not to lose your sight picture and trigger control in trying for speed. This will come later, with much practice, but if you start to sacrifice a good sight picture you will be losing ground. Another point is that the hurry-up to get off shots can quickly lead to yanking the trigger and flinching—both bad faults.

It will not take much work to build your speed up to the timed fire event—five shots in 20 seconds. When you reach this point and are scoring well, it is good to stop and work on it until you get the feel of the timing. If you have done well so far on slow fire, you will find that, surprisingly enough, the allotted time of four seconds for each shot is ample for you to recover from any movement, find your sight picture quickly, then have time enough for a fairly deliberate trigger let-off.

One of the secrets of getting out a properly spaced rapid fire string is to get the first shot off just as quickly as the targets face you (or time is called, with stationary targets). You should be ready to touch off as soon as the sight picture is right. This then leaves you almost 2½ seconds for each of the rest of four shots—and this is a big help.

If you use a revolver, it will be a double action because these models have adjustable sights—whereas single actions almost always have fixed sights—and because the accuracy potential of a double action is higher. But the double action will be fired as a single action in slow fire—that is, cocked manually before each shot; the accuracy a target shooter needs is impossible with the gun and sight movement that would result if he worked a double action through its trigger. But cocking the revolver before every shot will pose a problem in the timed and rapid fire sequences. It takes much practice and it may cause you to change your method of gripping the gun from that used in slow fire. You must hold the gun so that you can cock the hammer with a straight back movement of the thumb, while keeping the gun pointed at the target. It should not dip down or up or swing from side to side appreciably, or valuable time in picking up the sight picture again will be lost. This control in cocking the hammer is best learned through repeated practice in dry firing at home. In time, you will be cocking the gun without thinking about it. This is the goal to reach.

In the center-fire matches, you will probably start off with a .38 Special revolver in a match model. However, many target shooters avoid learning to cock a revolver hammer by shooting factory made target autos in .38 Special caliber or by using accurized versions of military model pistols. These all produce 10-ring accuracy and are favored by many shooters, even for the slow fire stages of the match.

When you first begin to shoot a center-fire, you will at once become aware that you need a firmer grip on the gun than with the .22. The revolver, particularly, needs a tight grip with the third, fourth, and fifth fingers to keep your hand in position after recoil, both for cocking the hammer and to maintain the same point of impact with the gun. Homework with a spring grip exerciser is the medicine to develop these muscles, but don't work hard with the trigger finger. This should retain its sensitivity.

Just as target rifle shooters pay special attention to the ammunition they use—demanding the best, most accurate ammo available—pistol targeteers are also a selective group. Like riflemen, many handgunners load their own ammo, at least for practice (in some competitions, there is a rule that selected lots

Here is a center-fire target revolver with typical target grips, adjustable sights, extra wide trigger, and wide hammer spur.

of factory loaded stuff must be used). Almost every handgunner, whether he buys or loads his cartridges, uses wadcutters in practice and in competition. Wadcutters are unjacketed lead bullets made especially for target shooting; they are almost cylindrical in shape as opposed to having the tapered nose of more conventional bullets. They are seated completely within the cartridge case, instead of sticking out as ordinary bullets do; this eliminates the chance of a bullet being damaged and having its accuracy impaired as it is fed from the magazine in an auto pistol. Since it uses less powder than conventional loads—both because it is seated deep in the case and because a light load is very accurate at handgun range—it is sometimes a trifle cheaper to use than hunting ammo. The light powder charge also produces less recoil, which is a factor that affects the shooter's ability to score bull's-eyes. And finally, it punches an almost perfectly round hole in target paper, which makes for ease in measuring group size and scoring.

Plastic or wax bullets are used for short range, and especially indoor, practice by pistol target shooters—and by more and more shooters of every variety in the few years since they were invented. These loads are the cheapest of all, and they don't present problems of noise, recoil, or danger to the surrounding

The center-fire target automatic in this photograph is factory built; other big bores used by target shooters are especially customized versions of the standard military .45.

On the right is a wadcutter bullet next to a conventional pistol cartridge into which this target bullet is loaded. Wadcutters are used by target shooters primarily because they are extremely accurate at short range and because they produce less recoil, a fact that helps shooters particularly in fast firing events.

area. They are powered by a primer only—no powder is necessary—and they are effective indicators of your accuracy within about 25 feet.

In the course of attending and firing in various matches, you will handle a number of different handguns: revolvers, autos, perhaps some single shots, and various calibers: .22, .38 Special, .45 Auto, .45 Auto Rim, and, perhaps, the .44 Special. You will find that each requires some slight difference in gripping, for no two shooters' hands are the same and the grips on the various guns are of different designs. However, you will find that the basic requirements remain the same: a firm hold on the gun, good trigger control, and a clear view of the sights. After this, it's practice—at home and on the range.

Every match competitor today shoots several different courses during a season. The standard and most used course is the National Match, in which the slow fire stage is shot at 50 yards and the timed and rapid fire events

The author is shown practicing with a Luger. Like government issue Colt autos, Lugers are better suited to military than target use but, again like government issue Colts though perhaps not to as great a degree, they can be accurized by a gunsmith and will then perform admirably on targets.

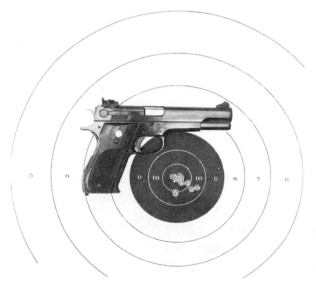

This fine Smith & Wesson Model 52 auto handles .38 Special midrange wadcutters and has adjustable target sights. The sharply delineated bullet holes in the target are characteristic of wadcutters —as is the evident accuracy.

This is a free pistol, used in international style events. It is an ultra-accurate single shot .22 with a special grip and finely adjustable sights and trigger pull.

from 25 yards. There are many other courses, but all include slow, timed, and rapid fire strings. The Camp Perry Course and the NRA Short Course are both fired at 25 yards for all three events, but the Perry permits only five minutes for 10 slow fire shots, while the NRA permits the more usual 10 minutes.

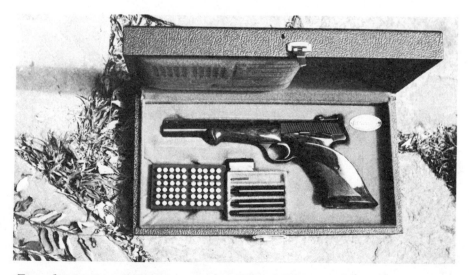

For a hangunner who wants to learn match shooting, no better start can be had than with a .22 autoloading pistol. Shown here is a fine Browning .22 with target sights.

Many shooters with long experience in American style shooting are varying their programs with international style events: the Olympic rapid fire and free pistol, international rapid fire and so on. The free (or match) pistol is an exceptionally accurate arm designed specifically for target shooting. It's a single shot .22 rim-fire pistol used in slow fire competition (usually at 50 meters). It has a finely adjustable trigger and a custom made, hand fitting grip with a thumb rest and a bottom projection or platform to support your hand. Holding this type of gun is almost like wearing a glove, and the muzzle seems like an extension of your arm, so aiming can be very precise. Moreover, the grip is sometimes adjustable—you can tighten it for a perfect fit. The sights on a free pistol are, naturally, of the target type with micrometer click adjustments for the rear one.

In general, all international shooting is a bit more demanding than our American match courses and, at any rate, it is different. The international slow fire target is smaller than ours and it is fired over a 50 meter course, which adds about three yards to our 50 yard range. And the international rapid fire program is even faster than ours—as fast as five shots in three seconds. The main thing for beginning target handgunners to remember, despite all of the different competitions that they may eventually qualify for, is that our American match program is tough enough for any beginner.

Chapter 11

HOW TO SHOOT IN THE FIELD

In field shooting, a hunter is not bound by formal rules of gun handling or shooting positions. The object is to kill the game quickly and neatly—with the first shot if possible. A high percentage of one-shot kills can be achieved by the use of certain techniques. First let's discuss those that pertain to the rifle; an experienced rifleman is sure to take every advantage he can before he touches off the trigger.

This means that if he is faced with a long shot he will quickly judge the range, "dope" the wind and the amount he needs to hold off for its sideward effect, then get into the steadiest possible position for the shot.

If the country is open and without high grass or other vegetation, he will look for a rest that he can use in the prone position. If there is no rock, hummock, log, or stump handy for such a rest, he will improvise, using a rolled up jacket, his spotting scope and its tripod turned sideways, his binocular case, or the glasses themselves stood on end. Lacking all of these aids, he will still shoot from the prone position and, if his rifle is so equipped, he will use a tight sling—which takes only a few seconds to put into use, as I'll explain in a moment.

But there are many situations in which the prone position cannot be used: where high grass or other obstructions block the view of the game just above ground level, where the hunter spies game as he is working down a slope and must shoot across to a far hillside, where he is in deep, soft snow, or where he doesn't have time enough to get set in the prone. These situations call for the sitting position, which is probably the most effective means of getting off a steady shot in all forms of rifle hunting, year in and year out, at all kinds of game in many different types of terrain.

You can get into the sitting position in a hurry. Just squat quickly, sit down, knees cocked up, facing about 45 degrees to the right of your line of proposed fire. Lean forward as you shoulder the rifle so that the flats of the upper arms just above the elbows are against the flat inner surfaces of the legs just below and inside the knees. With your heels dug in and your legs firmly planted,

The steadiest position for the rifleman in the field is prone, and if possible the thing to do is to find or improvise a rest for the rifle. A few of the more easily found rests are shown here. If none of these is available, however, and if no other possibilities present themselves, then shooting prone, even without a support, is the best thing to do.

Where the prone position cannot be used, the sitting position is the steadiest available to the shooter.

this gives a shooting platform that is almost as steady as the prone position, especially if a tight sling is used. If you have placed your legs properly to begin with, you will find that the left arm will rest firmly directly under the rifle in an almost vertical position, giving the steadiest possible hold. Sometimes it is possible to firm up the sitting position even more by dropping alongside a small tree, then resting the left or right shoulder against the trunk as you assume the position.

To get back to the sling—every rifle should have one and, for every kind of rifle hunting except in brush or timber, it should be a real shooting sling rather than just a carrying strap. Aside from its obvious use in carrying a rifle, the sling when properly adjusted is of the greatest aid in steadying your hold and helping a smooth trigger squeeze. It is a simple matter to adjust the loop to the correct length so that it will lock the left hand to the fore end of the rifle when used in the sitting or prone position. Properly adjusted, the sling, when tightened high up on the upper left arm and with the left hand passed around it and under the forearm, should hold the rifle snugly enough so that it can be placed against the right shoulder without any assist from the right hand. This means that your left hand will be jammed against the forward swivel with some force—and that's the way it should be.

The kneeling position is one I never use since, for me, it is barely better than offhand. When shooting game that's moving in cover, I prefer to take my chances on both feet so I can shift quickly if the need arises. So far, I have never found a situation in which I might kneel that I couldn't handle as well by sitting—and be a whole lot steadier. The kneeling position was adopted by the military centuries ago and is still used in target shooting, but it has no place in hunting.

Even in the sitting position, you can often find a prop to help steady you, such as the tree in these pictures. And as you can see, such a support can work on either your right or left side.

A sling is an invaluable aid, and it is something that every rifle, except one to be used exclusively for hunting in heavy cover, should have. You can slip into it in a few seconds, as the author shows, and it is useful in any shooting position.

The offhand position is the most difficult to shoot from, even if you use a sling. Here, too, you can use a tree for a rest, but note that you must change the position of your forward hand.

Without a sling, carrying strap, or tree to utilize as a rest, you can still improve your steadiness somewhat when firing from the offhand position by moving your left hand to grip at or near the front end of the rifle's forearm, or you can bring the left arm in to rest firmly against your side.

The offhand, or standing, position is one that demands endless practice, and few hunters devote enough time to it to become really skilled. Even in offhand shooting, you can sometimes get an assist from a nearby tree, using it as a prop for steadiness. If there's no branch at the right height, you can brace the palm of your forward hand flat against the tree trunk, cradling the forearm of your rifle between your thumb and fingers.

When nothing else offers support, and if your rifle isn't equipped with a sling but does have a carrying strap, you can make your stance a bit more solid by using a "hasty sling." This is simply a matter of slipping your left arm between the strap and the rifle, drawing the strap taut against the back of your biceps, just above your elbow. This creates countertension; the strap pulls down on the rifle's forearm, while your hand presses upward against it.

If your rifle has neither a sling nor a carrying strap, you can steady your hold somewhat by merely changing the grip of your non-shooting hand. Straighten your left arm so that your hand is farther forward than usual; some shooters actually lock the elbow and grip the very end of the rifle's forearm to get stability. Or you can pull your left arm in, resting it against your side.

The point to repeat is that in field shooting you must take every possible advantage of a sling or natural aids to improvise a rest. It is certainly no less sporting to kill an animal from a rest position than from the offhand.

SHOOTING A RIFLE IN TIMBER

When you hunt elk or deer—whitetail in particular—you do most of your shooting in heavy cover such as second growth, hardwoods, lodgepole pine, spruce, and fir. There is no more difficult rifle shooting than this because the target is invariably obscured—at least partially—by trees and brush. Here a knowledge of anatomy really pays off. (See Chapter 12 for an analysis of vital target areas.) You can decide on the best shot to make if you can see some part of your quarry's body, even though much of the animal is hidden by trees, leaves, and brush.

A timber hunter must always be ready to get off a quick, properly held shot, for his target shifts very quickly with the animal's slightest movement. For example, a whitetail moving along a runway, feeding slowly or just traveling, seldom offers the same vital spot for two consecutive seconds. If you find an opening in the screening timber ahead of the animal, first his head and neck will poke through—perhaps long enough for you to make a spine shot. Yet the animal may move just enough, as you get ready to squeeze off, to conceal the head and neck but bring the shoulder area into view; then you must shift to this new target before the animal passes from view completely. Fix the vital areas in your mind so that you can pick them out instantly as the target shifts. Often a hunter is ready to make good a chest cavity shot but isn't fast enough to get it off before the hindquarters move into view. He may then pull the trigger and hope. It is usually a vain hope—ending in wounded but lost game.

It is equally foolish to shoot *through* heavy brush and second growth. A slow, heavy bullet will carry through some leaves and twigs, but the typical high velocity deer slug usually breaks into bits when it strikes a sapling more than an inch in diameter. Even if part of the bullet gets through, the chances are heavily against its inflicting a mortal wound. Judging when to shoot and when not to is very important; you must know how much vegetation you can plow through with your rifle and bullet type. If you can't poke a bullet through an opening, pass up the shot and hope for a better break in a few moments or on the next buck.

RUNNING SHOTS IN TIMBER

Shooting at running game in timber is usually futile; it merely adds to the total of wounded, dead, and unrecovered game each year. A running animal has usually been frightened by the hunter and is heading directly away from him, showing only the hindquarters. A man must have little regard for humane hunting practices to attempt such a shot.

However, driven game or, occasionally, game jumped by the hunter will offer a broadside or quartering shot at close range. The only possible chance for a *clean* hit in this situation is to keep your wits about you long enough to find an opening *ahead* of the animal, throw your sights there and touch off the shot as the animal appears, giving it a short lead of perhaps a foot—just as you would with a shotgun. Trying to keep your sights on an animal as it moves through timber, firing shot after shot until it passes from view, is extremely unproductive. If there is no opening in the cover, learn to wait; a running animal frequently will stop just before passing from view, giving you a chance for a good shot.

LONG RANGE RIFLE SHOOTING

Hunting in the open plains and prairie country or in high mountain areas demands long shots—200 yards or more as a rule. Two factors are important in this kind of shooting: knowing the trajectory of your rifle (having sighted-in at the longest "point-blank" range) and knowing the effect of wind drift. The so-called flat shooting cartridges shoot flat only in rifles that have been properly sighted-in at long range. With most rifles this means having your point of aim not less than 200 yards away, and shooting the highest velocity cartridges; 300 yards is an even better point-blank range. (The term "point-blank" simply means that the rifle is zeroed to hit where it is aimed with no hold-over or hold-under.) Such sighting-in gives you the maximum effect of flat trajectory: the bullet strikes only a few inches high at shorter ranges, yet drops only a few inches at the longest practical hunting distances. This means that your judgment of range need not be so precise and that you need not calculate hold-over or hold-under so closely.

Wind drift must always be considered in long range shooting if there is even a perceptible breeze. The required amount of "hold-off" into the wind varies enormously with the caliber, the bullet weight and shape, the speed and direction of the wind, and the range. It's a good idea to get specific information on wind drift for your particular cartridge and load; the figures are generally available from ammo makers. Some of the high velocity, flat trajectory, long range loads—for example, the .222 and .224—are more wind sensitive than the average cartridge.

Only your judgment of wind velocity will tell you the amount to hold off into the wind to make hits at long range on a still target, whether it's a small varmint or a big game animal. For example, if you are trying for a woodchuck at 300 yards with a .243 rifle firing an 80 grain bullet, and you feel only a faint movement of air on your left cheek, you should hold your scope crosshairs on the left outline of the chuck's body. If the wind is noticeable, let's call it a breeze, your hold to the left will be a full width of the chuck's body. If the wind is still stiffer than this, you must hold off even more, sometimes up to 24 inches, to allow for the drift of the bullet as it journeys to the target. This is all a matter of judgment based on experience.

Quite often you will get a good clue on wind drift and bullet drop at long range if you can see the spot where your last shot hit, where it kicked up dust, rock chips, or snow. If you're sighting through a scope at these ranges, which is most likely, recoil will blot out your view of the target for your shooting eye. This is another instance, therefore, where it is important to keep your left eye open when shooting, for with this eye you will be able to see a miss and make corrections on your next shot—if the animal stays put.

Another (though less important) factor in long range shooting is the amount of "drop" to figure when you fire uphill or downhill. Normally, this difference in trajectory is insignificant at hunting ranges and angles. However, the rule of thumb is that a rifle always shoots somewhat *higher* when the target is at a noticeable angle from the horizontal, and *it makes no difference whether the target is above the shooter or below him.* The point of impact

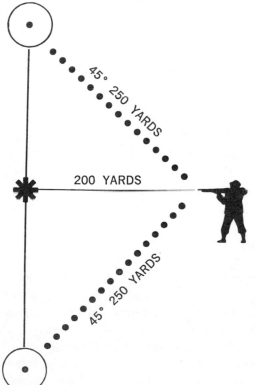

200 YARDS

You must hold low for either an uphill or a downhill shot, common misconceptions to the contrary. This diagram shows that the "gravity distance," the horizontal line along which gravity is exerted on your bullet, is shorter than your line of sight, and to compensate for the fact that your rifle will therefore shoot a bit high, you must hold under your target.

is slightly high in both uphill and downhill shooting. In either case, the effect of gravity requires you to hold low.

To understand this, you must realize that the force of gravity is exerted along a horizontal plane (from your rifle to a point directly above or below the target, depending on whether you're shooting uphill or downhill). This "gravity distance" is *shorter* than the line of sight between you and the game standing above or below you, so you must hold low for your bullet to drop enough to hit.

A steady position is vital at long range, and you usually have time enough to get set. Any one of the rests we've talked about will work in one of these situations, but prone shooting is by far the most accurate.

RUNNING SHOTS IN THE OPEN

In open country, shooting a rifle at moving game is not much different from shooting a flying bird with a shotgun—you simply have to be more accurate in aiming and judging the lead. This takes lots of practice and here the Western hunter has a big edge: he has plenty of jack rabbits all year around for moving targets. The best that the rest of the riflemen hunters can get elsewhere is another species, the cottontail, which does almost as well except you won't find him often in the open. All hunters should use the running deer target—one that travels across an open area on rope and pulleys —for off-season practice.

To hit a moving animal with a rifle bullet, you use the same system you use with a shotgun—you lead it. If you don't, you won't hit it. At short range, you would take a much smaller lead than with a shotgun because of the vastly greater speed of a bullet over that of a charge of shot. However, in open country you will be shooting at distances much longer than you would be if using a shotgun, so the actual leads become somewhat similar.

You will handle the rifle in shooting at a moving animal just as you do your shotgun. You swing with the target, pass it, keep swinging ahead until you have the right lead, then quickly squeeze off the shot. As in shotgun shooting, your reaction time and the ignition time of the rifle cause an interval in getting the bullet to the target. You will quickly discover this when you first shoot at running game. A typical example would be in making a shot at an antelope, say, 200 yards away, running at 40 miles an hour directly across your line of fire. If your swing is good and you keep your rifle moving as you fire, you will need about two lengths of the animal to connect with it in the chest area—a lead of about eight feet. On quartering shots you will take less lead, still less if the animal is not running at full speed. Only practice

The running deer target simulates a deer's movement; practicing on one of these sharpens your eye for shots at a fast moving animal.

on moving targets will give you the clue as to your swing, reaction time, and, thus, the correct amount of lead.

The scope sight with crosshair reticle is undoubtedly the best sighting equipment for shooting moving game at 100 yards or more. In use, you lay the horizontal wire along the animal's body, then move the rifle so that the vertical wire is ahead just enough to give you the right amount of lead. It is much easier to do this with a scope than with iron sights and easier to do it with a crosshair than with a post or a dot reticle. You can also better estimate elevation with the crosshair than with any other sighting device on a rifle.

Of all the larger game animals, antelope are probably the easiest to hit on the move because they are usually running over fairly flat country and they run smoothly with the body parallel to the ground, not bouncing up and down in the typical gait of a whitetail or mule deer. Making a vital hit on a bounding deer at fairly long range takes not only keen shooting but a large slice of luck.

HANDLING THE RIFLE

We noted, in Chapter 1, comfortable ways to carry a rifle in the field. Review those now if it is necessary. And remember, a firearm should always be carried with the safety on or with the hammer in the safety notch when a live shell is chambered. The safety should not be snapped off or the hammer cocked until the rifle is raised to shoot. And *never* carry a rifle over a fence with you; put it on the other side before you go over.

In horseback hunting, your rifle should be carried in a saddle scabbard, *always* with the chamber empty. There's time enough to operate the action to load it after you pull the rifle from the scabbard. A bucking horse or a spill down a slope can cause disaster if you carry a ready to fire rifle.

Timber hunters must constantly bear in mind that they're not alone in the woods. In the excitement of spotting a moving animal, make sure you're

Never carry a rifle over or through a fence with you. Instead, put it on the other side and then climb over.

aiming at legal game and not at another hunter. The utmost care must also be exercised in shooting at game on a drive. Each stander or watcher (the hunter to whom the game is being driven; the shooter) must know exactly where the other standers are and must avoid taking shots at game crossing the position of other standers. The same thing applies to the drivers who are moving game toward the stands; they must not shoot, and the men on stands must be careful not to take any shots that might endanger them. Driving game can be hazardous if every member of the hunting party isn't continuously alert to the danger of random shooting.

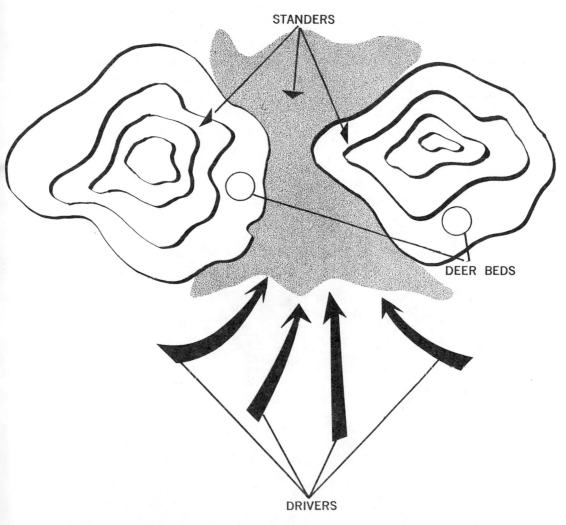

Here is a diagram of a typical deer drive, showing positions of the drivers and standers and illustrating a most important safety point: no shots should be taken that might possibly endanger other hunters.

HUNTING WITH THE HANDGUN

You may remember that in Chapter 9 we praised handguns with adjustable rear sights, because a six o'clock hold gives you the best sight picture for target work but not always for hunting. By lowering your rear sight, you can put your area of aim directly on your front sight, rather than above it. This places the sight against the center of the target, not underneath as in the six o'clock hold. The maximum effective range of most handguns is 50 yards, so your target isn't far off. Sighting with this lowering "center hold" is faster than trying to get an exact six o'clock sight picture.

Recent developments in handgun cartridges for long range shooting, in combination with scope sights, have considerably increased the effective range of the varmint and big game hunter who uses these sidearms. Handgun scopes, while they offer little or no magnification, do clarify the target. And with one reticle—crosshair—as opposed to front and rear sights, they eliminate the need to maintain the hard to hold sight alignment and picture needed when you shoot a typical handgun. Kills with scope sighted high velocity small bores on varmints and with scoped .357, .41, and .44 Magnums and the newer .30 Herrett (for which a Contender pistol barrel is chambered) on big game are made at ranges well over 100 yards. These guns have the accuracy to make vital hits, and the scope makes such accuracy possible. The .22 Jet, .221 Fireball, .256 Magnum, and the three larger Magnums have velocity enough for flat trajectory, taking much guesswork out of long range shooting. With a scoped handgun zeroed at 100 yards, it's possible to make kills at almost twice that yardage with relatively little hold-over for bullet drop at long range, but *this requires very steady hands and a firm shooting position.*

Here is a scoped handgun of the type used by hunters. Between the development of long range pistol cartridges and scope sights for handguns, the range at which the pistol hunter can shoot effectively has been greatly increased.

Because shooting a handgun is inherently more difficult than shooting a shoulder arm, you should avoid field shooting in the classic one hand target stance. Utilize a support when possible, and use two hands to steady the gun.

Here are three recommended field shooting positions for the hand gunner. You can see from these photos that there are no formal rules; the object is to assume the steadiest position you can for each shot, using part of the terrain for prop where possible, or other part of your body as a support for your shooting hand.

The prone position for handgun shooting, as with a rifle, is the steadiest. But here, too, try to find a support and use two hands.

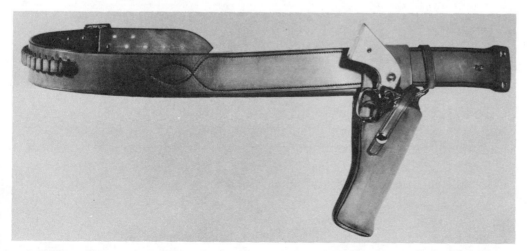

A handgun holster for field use should be worn high on the hip, where this model rides, and should have a flap or strap to hold the gun securely when you're moving about.

The comparatively great waver that is present in handgun shooting has been stressed before and should be stressed again. When you're in the field, your goal is to kill game efficiently and humanely—you're not just practicing. Therefore, offhand shots should be avoided. If you absolutely can't find any sort of rest, *use both hands*. Grip your gun with your shooting hand in the standard manner, but rest this hand in your non-shooting hand.

You can almost always sit down, whether or not there's a support handy, for added stability. Some hunters rest both arms on their knees. Others claim to get rocklike steadiness by wrapping their arms *around* their knees; the outward pressure of your legs will steady your gun if you lock your hands together. Some lean back, propped up on one hand, with one knee bent; you can use this knee platform as a rest, too.

If the ground is flat you can also steady yourself by utilizing the prone position, holding the gun directly in front of you, with your non-shooting hand again working as a support. You will do even better by using a support—a boulder, a tree limb, or your folded up jacket on the ground if nothing better presents itself.

A word about handgun accessories is in order here. Low slung holsters may be all right for fast draw practice, but they have no place in hunting. All they accomplish as a rule is to catch in the brush, get tipped sideways by boulders and get in the way when you're crawling. A handgun is a valuable tool and you certainly don't want yours falling out of its holster. You'll be much better off hunting with a holster worn high on the hip, with a flap or strap to hold the gun in place.

One more word about handgun hunting: don't carry a live shell in the chamber. Cocking the gun will chamber a round, so why court danger?

HUNTING WITH THE SHOTGUN

The lessons you learned with the hand trap and on the trap and skeet fields won't complete your wildfowling education. Shooting ducks and geese takes lead and follow-through that must be precise, particularly when you pass shoot at long range. The ability to lead these fast fliers comes only with experience.

It's likely that no one ever missed wildfowl by overleading. The temptation is always to shorten the lead, for it is difficult to believe so long a lead is needed; if you're missing ducks or geese, try shooting twice as far ahead of them as you think you should, and watch what happens.

It's different with upland game, however. Everything you learned on the practice field with clay birds is put to hunting use now. The problem is that the shooter must cope with a target that appears at an unpredictable range, speed, and angle.

You must therefore be prepared for anything. Learn to mount and swing your gun smoothly, touching off the trigger without conscious effort, concentrating only on the target. Complete familiarity with your gun is essential. Most important with upland birds, you must determine their line of flight before you commit yourself by throwing your gun up. Once you've started on a specific line of movement, there is seldom time to change direction.

Shotgun shooting takes a complex, coordinated movement of eyes, hands—in fact, the entire body. If a bird bursts away in a direction that puts you in an awkward position, you have to shift your feet and body so that you can mount your gun smoothly. With practice, you can learn to do this in such a fluid motion that you synchronize the rhythm of your body, hands, and eyes with the bird's flight.

The trick of leading a bird—or even a rabbit—is something you should have already mastered as a result of your clay bird practice. However, you'll find new and disconcerting situations in bird shooting that you didn't encounter in practice. All too often grouse, quail, and woodcock disappear in a flash behind a screen of brush or timber. If you're cool and quick enough, you'll learn to swing with the line of flight, point just ahead of the bird, and fire as you keep swinging. Frequently, your pattern will drive through the screening leaves to drop the bird, even though he disappeared from sight.

The best game shotgunners swing and lead in one motion, then fire. The fast swinger requires only a minimum of lead in upland shooting, for the continued movement of the gun as he fires maintains his lead. "Snap shooting," in which the gunner picks a spot somewhere ahead of his target and tries to place his pattern there, demands precision calculation that few men can ever learn. A much greater lead is required, and that complicates the whole situation. The best plan is to remember the lessons you learned during your practice sessions with clay targets and apply them in the field.

A good field shot—especially a bird hunter—is ready to mount his gun instantly from any position, and in any direction that game may demand. In tramping through brush and weeds he is always alert for the sudden appearance of game and he tries to avoid getting off balance as he ducks and weaves through cover. His body must be ready to swing and pivot in almost any direction and at any time; this is not always possible, but it is rare for him to be caught off balance and unprepared to mount his gun when a bird appears. His ear is always cocked for the sound of a flushing bird, whether it is the wing-whistle of a woodcock, the drumming rustle of a grouse, or the buzz of a quail. His reactions are geared to the sounds that reach his ears and an accomplished gunner is usually moving his firearm in the direction of the flush sound before he actually sees the bird.

In Chapter 1 we talked about various methods of carrying your shotgun

We've talked about it before with rifles, but the same thing holds true for shotguns: they should be put on the other side of a fence before you go over.

and how to shoulder it quickly. Now is the time to review these carries and to practice them so that you can mount your gun surely and rapidly. And regardless of any advice you've heard about how to hold your gun when climbing over or through a fence, the safest practice is to put your gun on the other side first and not hold it at all while climbing.

You must also guard against shooting at low flying birds or at furred game if you're not dead certain of the location of every other member of your hunting party—including the dogs. And your shotgun must *always* be carried with its safety on. Shotgun safeties are conveniently located and can be thrown off with the thumb or trigger finger during the mounting procedure. There is no excuse for carrying a shotgun with the safety off; it's best not to go afield until you can snap it off without conscious effort as you are raising your gun to fire.

With the exception of some large game birds, as we will note in the next chapter, and big game when hunted with a smoothbore loaded with rifled slugs or buckshot, shotgun hunters are not required to have as precise a knowledge of the anatomy of their game as riflemen. A shot charge is by no means selective; it spreads. What is important is to know your gun's killing pattern— the percentage of shot it puts into a target zone—with each shot size and load you plan to use. The shotgun is by no means a long range arm and beginners are often tempted to take chances at a distant bird when there's no hope of making a clean kill. Exert every effort to get the gun up as quickly as possible and make a killing shot while the game is still well within range—and that usually means no more than 40 yards.

Chapter 12

HOW TO KILL GAME

Since the essence of sportsmanship in the field—aside from being a gentleman —is to kill your game neatly and mercifully with the first shot, several factors become involved. One is a basic knowledge of the anatomy of the animals you hunt, especially with a rifle or handgun. Another is choosing a gun and ammunition combination, whether you'll be using rifle, pistol, or shotgun, that has been proven effective. The third factor is, naturally, the ability to shoot well.

In the previous chapter we went into considerable detail on *how* to place a bullet where you want it. Here we will go into *where* to place it and *what loads* to use.

A most important point is to develop the concept of picking out or visualizing a target area on your game. In some 40 years of hunting, I have killed thousands of game birds and animals of all sizes and, in the course of adhering to the philosophy of one shot kills, I have developed a system of sorts that helps do the job.

This is a relatively easy matter with small game animals; the power of modern firearms and loads usually enables you to kill a small animal quickly by placing a bullet anywhere in the forward half of its body.

THE VITAL AREAS IN BIG GAME

In bigger animals the system I mentioned comes into play. When I shoot at a deer, an elk, or a moose, I am not thinking of the game as a whole; rather, I concentrate on one-third of the animal's torso as my target in almost all cases. The center of the body mass is dismissed. In fact, I forget that the animal has a paunch or hindquarter area. I center my vision on the shoulder area—the forward section of the spinal column, the chest cavity—and pinpoint

The outlines of all hoofed big game animals are similar. This is a whitetail deer.

this, and this alone, for my target. This is how you must think and react when game suddenly appears.

More frequently than not, you will get a chance at a big game animal that offers a difficult angle for placing the bullet. Sometimes you can wait a bit for the animal to move, offering perhaps a better opening for a killing shot, but often you won't have the time for this. You must make a quick decision to shoot *right now* or to pass up the chance. In this spot, your visual concept of where to hit the animal is vital; your bullet must strike the spot "where he lives."

You can pinpoint this spot pretty much in the same way a matador picks the spot for his killing thrust—directly between the shoulder blades and fore-legs. This is the area of life in *any* animal, and if you fix this in your mind, you can almost always make it your target area. At the top of this is the spine, and a deadly shot that breaks the spine is one made broadside, with the bul-

Here is a bull elk; his chest, shoulder and neck are the best spots to hit in order to assure yourself of a clean kill.

Most large animals are amazingly strong, and therefore are difficult to knock down. This is especially true of a big bull moose. You must put your first shot into the vital area if the game isn't to escape.

let placed well up in the front shoulder area. Here the spine dips down between the shoulder blades. A high shot in this section breaks down one shoulder, crushes the spine, and drops the animal instantly. If the bullet is heavy enough and holds together well, it will pass through and break the far, or off, shoulder, too. It's a recommended shot to use on a big bear when your primary interest is to drop him on the spot and keep him down. In fact, on any dangerous game this is a most effective bullet placement and it should always be made if you have a choice.

The chest cavity, however, is the largest target area affording a quick kill, and it is therefore the choice of most big game hunters. The life of every animal is centered there, in the rib cage—that area lying between the forelegs and the diaphragm. There lies the compact package of heart and lungs, and if your bullet destroys any appreciable amount of these vital tissues, your animal hasn't long to live.

When you get a broadside shot, your bullet should be aimed at the top of the front leg. Since the heart and lungs are low down in the chest cavity, such a hit—made with a properly expanding bullet—inflicts massive damage. Even if your bullet strikes somewhat to the rear, missing the heart, it will certainly kill almost as quickly by rupturing lung tissue. Before a bullet collapses them, the lungs are larger than the heart, and a shot in this area is deadly. While a lung shot animal rarely drops immediately upon being hit— the reason for shooting through the shoulders to anchor game that might charge—he seldom goes very far before the chest cavity fills with blood, literally drowning him.

Naturally, bullet placement depends very much on the attitude the animal presents to you. If you have a full view of the game, broadside shots are the easiest, and of these, lung shots are easier than spine shots. If your target is quartering away, the bullet should be aimed to enter at the back ribs and penetrate forward through the rib cage. An easy rule to remember for quartering away shots is to aim in a line with the off shoulder; you won't be able to see this shoulder, but you will know its exact location if you've taken the trouble to find out about the anatomy of the game you're hunting.

A head-on shot offers a tempting target. A hit square in the middle of the brisket, well up into the juncture of the neck, is most effective in destroying rib cage vitals. If the animal offers a head-on shot but is quartering, the fast, easy choice is to place the bullet where the neck joins the shoulder. If your bullet strikes a bit low, you'll wreck heart and lungs; if your hold is a trifle high, you'll break the spine and destroy lung tissue. Both are deadly hits.

The other vital spots are, of course, the neck and head—both relatively small targets and much easier to miss than the shoulder and chest cavity. We can virtually eliminate the head shot for the obvious reason that the kind of bullet normally used in hunting will make a sorry mess of a trophy head. Moreover, the head is a comparatively small target and is usually moving.

A shot through the neck, aimed at the spine, gives the neatest kill of all if you're shooting a rifle of ample power—and *if* you break the spine. On deer, this shot is deadly because of its paralyzing effect even if the spine is not broken; however, when you try this shot on bull elk or moose, whose necks become thickened during the rut, you'd better be sure to use a powerful load and hit the spinal column. Only a few experts try for a spine shot in the neck, because of the risk of overshooting.

No one should shoot at a game animal that is moving rapidly directly away. This is inhumane and wasteful. If the game is moving away at a slight angle, you can put a bullet through the ham or the back end of the flank toward the lung area. But you should have a powerful rifle and cartridge if you try this. And you'll also need a bullet with great penetrating potential if you try to take an animal that is standing still but facing directly away from you. For this shot, your aiming point is through the center of the pelvis, and the bullet will go forward into the lung area.

You can see that a knowledge of the anatomy of the animals you are hunting is invaluable, and the "between the forelegs" area will do the best job of humane killing. The rule of thumb for beginners in big game hunting is to aim every shot at the forward third of an animal. A shot placed well forward will break the shoulder, rupture the spine, or destroy vital rib cage tissue. A bullet placed anywhere to the rear of the rib cage probably will not result in a humane kill; you will need to follow the game and finish it off—if you can find it.

You can improve your chances of making a one shot kill by using the information I have given you, by learning something about the anatomy of the animals you are hunting, by knowing your rifle and the ammunition in it, and by practicing on a deer profile target which is available from sporting goods stores and can be rigged at almost any target range.

THE ANATOMY OF LARGE BIRDS

In shooting the larger game birds—pheasants, geese, and wild turkey—you should restrict your area of concentration as you do on big game animals. The pheasant, particularly, has a lot of his length taken up by a long tail. If you use the center of his silhouette as a target, you will often find that your shot charge clips tail feathers and nothing else. Much the same can be said for geese and turkey, which have long necks that can affect your judgment of lead. In flight, I think of these birds as a head only and use the head as my point of reference in leading them. This gives me a much better chance to put shot into the head and neck—which downs these birds better than shot scattered over the whole body area.

Birds with long necks, such as geese and wild turkey, present a problem in judging lead. For these, use the head as an aiming point and you stand a better chance of putting pellets into the head and neck area.

When shooting pheasant, concentrate on putting your shot charge into the forward one-third of the body. If you try for the center, you'll wind up wasting a lot of the effectiveness of your pellets on the bird's long tail.

In this connection, it should be repeated that the *smallest* size of shot that you can depend on to give penetration at normal range will be the most effective in making hits in head and neck, because you are throwing many more pellets of small shot than you would be if you used larger shot. A load of #7½ for pheasant and #4 for geese and turkey are deadly killers *if* you use them within the limit of their maximum range and don't take chances on making a lucky hit.

BULLET WEIGHTS AND TYPES

Similarly, the bullet weight you choose for big game and varmints is an essential part of killing the game. The ideal of bullet performance is to create the maximum shock that the cartridge's basic energy can deliver—meaning that the bullet should remain in the animal's body. Quite often, in skinning out deer or other big game animals, I have found the bullet, well expanded, resting against the skin on the far side of the body. This is perfect bullet performance, since the slug penetrated the entire body and delivered its full potential of energy within the animal.

Some hunters will argue that a bullet should pass entirely through the animal to leave a better blood trail. It is my conviction that any bullet that passes through an animal wastes a certain amount of its energy—i.e., the foot pounds of striking force that are dissipated upon trees, rocks, or the ground *after* the bullet leaves the animal's body. I prefer to have a bullet stay in the animal, delivering its full potential of shock. When a bullet does this, you will usually not need to worry about a blood trail—at least not for more than a few yards.

How can we match bullet to animal to get these results? No choice is infallible, but the rule is: light bullets for small and medium sized game, heavy bullets for big game. We can carry this further by choosing bullets with thin jackets for small animals, heavy jackets (giving so-called controlled expansion) for big game. A prime example of a bullet designed for deepest penetration yet offering good forward (nose of bullet) expansion is the Nosler, a bullet used by hand loaders, which is a three piece unit having an "H" shaped jacket. Lead cores are swaged (compressed) into the upper and lower sections of the "H" with a lead tip exposed in the upper section. This upper, or forward, section mushrooms upon impact but the rear half of the bullet

Here are three popular big game bullets. From left to right they are the Winchester-Western Silvertip, Remington Corelokt and Winchester-Western Power-Point. The reason for the popularity of these loads is that they all offer controlled expansion—the front end of each mushrooms, opening a large wound channel and imparting a high degree of shock to the animal—while the rear portion retains its original diameter, pushing the bullet forward for maximum penetration.

stays at its original diameter to push onward for maximum penetration.

Modifications of this bullet are the Remington Corelokt and Winchester-Western Silvertip and Power-Point. These have extra-heavy jackets on the rear section of the bullet, which generally prevents much expansion. The front end opens up or peels back to create a large wound channel and deliver a high degree of shock.

In certain calibers you will find that the heaviest bullet weights are designed for animals larger than deer. For example, the .30/06 with 220 grain bullet and the .308 with 200 grain bullet will rarely open up enough to stay within the relatively small body of a deer. In most cases these heavy bullets, with their thick jackets, don't meet enough resistance to expand; they zip right on through, creating only a narrow wound channel and transmitting relatively

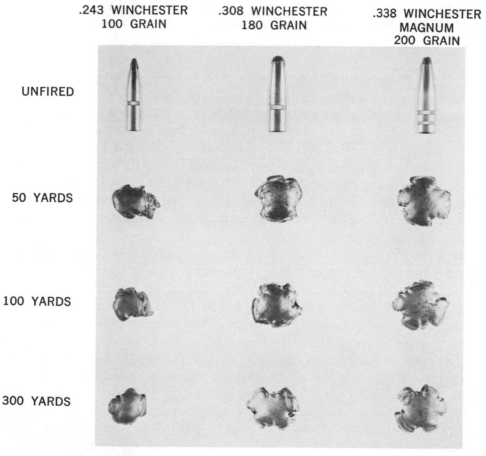

These pictures of Winchester-Western Power-Point bullets show the expansion they are capable of at various ranges.

Here are three small game and varmint cartridges. The one at left is loaded with a solid point bullet, which does not expand; this is for plinking or target shooting. In the center is a hollow point, used for small game shooting; this bullet will expand, although the expansion is not as closely controlled as in big game bullets. At the right is an expanding soft point bullet in a varmint cartridge; this slug will expand upon impact, and this type or a hollow point is used for varmint shooting.

low shock to the animal. I once finished off a large whitetail buck that had been wounded by another hunter. He had fired three .30/06 220 grain bullets through the deer's chest cavity, broadside. The buck would certainly have dropped shortly, but he had plenty of speed left as he passed me, about 200 yards from where he had been hit. Upon looking him over, I found three exit holes—barely larger than the entrance holes. The bullets had passed through without expanding to any degree, and the small exit holes let out very little blood for trailing. There was a good chance that a tenderfoot hunter, unfamiliar with trailing a wounded animal in dry leaves over hard ground, would have lost this buck.

It is therefore absolutely essential that you select wisely in regard to bullet weight and design. The trouble is that you must know something about the power potential of your cartridge, since in some calibers the heavy bullets are for deer size game; in others, the lighter bullets are for the deer size animals. A typical example would be the .243 Winchester, which is factory loaded with 80 grain or 100 grain bullets. Here the deer bullet weight is the 100 grain; the 80 grain is for varmints. Yet, with the .270 Winchester, loaded with either 100, 130, or 150 grain factory bullets, the 130 grain performs best on deer. The 100 grain bullet is the varmint load; the 150 grain for game larger than deer: elk or moose, where high penetration is demanded of *any* bullet. As close as you can come to a rule in this area is that if heavier bullets are available, they should be used for the largest game that can sensibly be hunted with that caliber.

For small game and varmints, the matter of bullet construction is much simplified. The .22s are either solid or hollow point bullets, and the popular varmint cartridges are hollow points or expanding soft points. In all small game hunting you will get maximum effect by using the hollow points, for the same reason you get this effect when using expanding bullets for big game. The solids are generally used for plinking and target shooting.

A chapter such as this is difficult to organize since the whole theory and practice of killing game is built of scattered bits of information, all important, yet composed of many factors. You must know animal anatomy, and you should know how your particular rifle performs on animal tissue with different loads, how to dope the wind and range for long shots into the vitals, and how to judge the location of the vital area on a big game animal even if most of its body is obscured by leaves, grass, or brush and if the angle is difficult. In wingshooting, you must know a great variety of leads since shots at game birds will offer you an almost infinite variety of angles.

DECEPTIVE LEADS

In Chapter 7 we dealt with a number of specific instances in wingshooting where the correct lead is important. To this we can add one big point in making clean kills: always give your bird a bit *more* lead than you would in shooting at a clay target. On any angle shot where you must lead noticeably to connect, the bird's head and neck are well ahead of his body, which is your target center—and I am thinking now of the smaller birds such as woodcock, quail, grouse, etc. The point is that you will never (or very seldom) *overlead* any bird and, even if only the fringe of your pattern makes contact, these shots will hit the head and neck area for a quick kill. Further, since every shot charge strings out in flight, just as water streams from a hose, even though some of the front part of the charge passes in front of the bird, he will be likely to fly into the balance of the shot string bringing up the rear half of the charge.

Leads above and below on game birds are another factor that should be considered, although few upland gunners do. Most birds, when flushed, are climbing to get elevation to clear brush or tall ground vegetation. You must hold over these birds to make a clean kill. If you do not, the top fringe of your pattern will connect with the lower part of the body, taking out some tail feathers and putting a few shot into the abdominal cavity. You might see feathers drifting down after your shot, but usually the bird keeps on going. Keep your pattern well above the climbing birds and they will fly into it.

The reverse situation is true when a grouse flushes from a tree well above ground. Although his flight line may be perfectly parallel with the ground, this line will always be at a falling angle to you and your gun. You must hold *under* these birds to connect. I can recall many kills I have made on grouse flushing from tall white pines, almost above me, when I could see three feet of air under the bird and over my gun muzzle.

HUNTING NERVES

The final and most important point in killing game is the hunter's emotional response at the moment. Every hunter, no matter how long and varied his experiences in killing game, becomes charged up when the chance to take his trophy arrives. His heart beats faster, his hands may shake a bit, and his breathing becomes labored. With this sort of physical disturbance, it is not easy to do everything just right. Your hold may not be precise, your trigger squeeze may be a bit hasty—and instead of making a clean hit, you either miss entirely or just wound the animal.

For this there is no real cure. Every hunter carries on the sport for the excitement, the thrill he gets from finding the game, stalking it, and making the kill. The tension can be nerve shattering until the animal is down for keeps. Yet, it is possible to get all the thrills that taking game has to offer and still do an efficient job of execution. The only approach is to develop confidence in your shooting ability, to know that you have the power in your hands to kill the animal, and to be certain that you have the skill to put that power where it belongs. It is *only* this assurance of your own capabilities, engendered by much shooting experience, that brings about the clean, merciful kills every hunter hopes to make and, in fairness to the game, *must* make if the sport is to survive.

During many years of hunting over the North American continent, I have lost one head of big game, wounded and unrecovered. This was a big bull elk that we had stalked to his bed. He spooked and left in high gear through thick lodgepole pine before I could get on him with the sights. Foolishly, I snapped off one shot as he bounded through the timber, head up and tilted back so that the long sweep of his antlers lined his flanks. I did swing ahead of him, through a foot-wide passage in the trees, and fired just below his thick neck. The bullet caught him somewhere, probably low in the neck or forward in the brisket. He did not pause in his flight. We picked up a blood trail shortly but this soon petered out. We spent the entire day hunting for him without success. I suspect that he was wounded lightly enough to recover, but I still think more about this animal than any I have killed.

Chapter 13

HOW TO SELECT YOUR GUN

The first firearms were simple devices whose sole purpose was to inflict lethal wounds on the anatomy of the human being. The early hand cannon was crude and forthright in design, a simple tube of metal carried in the hand, charged with black powder and a projectile, then fired by inserting a glowing match into a hole in the side of the tube's rear end. The projectile was discharged, with a great flash and roar, in the general direction of the foe.

From the era of this elementary firearm until today, gun development has moved, though without any coherent pattern, toward the firearm designed for special purposes. A century ago, a man might own a rifle big enough to kill deer or larger game, a shotgun for small game and a pistol for defense of person and household. The modern gun lover and sportsman is not content with such simplicity. Today we have, at the bottom of the scale, the little .22 caliber plinking rifle for fun and practice firing or to shoot a rabbit or squirrel. Then we find, moving up, the varmint rifle of modest range, perhaps a .222 for chuck shooting in farmlands. There are more powerful rifles for open country varmint shooting, guns that can also double for use on bigger game at long range, say the .243 or the 6mm Remington. And then, the well equipped hunter has a handy short range rifle for hunting deer in timber. If he's an Easterner, this might be a .30/30 carbine, a light .308, or the little .44 carbine. If he's a Western mountain hunter, he will insist on a rifle powerful enough to take elk and moose in timber, which means something in the class of the .338 Winchester or other popular Magnums.

And then, to run out the string to a logical conclusion for big game hunting, he might well have a powerful, long range bolt action rifle in .300 or .338 Magnum, which will drop the largest of North American animals at the longest practical hunting ranges.

This quick run-down will give you an idea of current specialization in rifles.

We could run off another list of shotguns and handguns and add a few rifles and scatterguns designed specifically for target shooting. You can see how versatile an arsenal the modern outdoorsman can build.

Specialization is the key word today in choosing the firearm for *any* purpose. The list of guns on the American market is staggering, in numbers, in types, and in bore sizes. Even recognized authorities in the field rarely agree completely as to the best gun for any one type of shooting, so the beginner is naturally somewhat puzzled when it comes to picking the right one.

Actually, this phenomenon of specialization has developed to the point where much overlapping and duplication exist. For example, the practical difference between a .270 and a .280, between a .308 and a .30/06, between a .243 and a 6mm Remington, is purely academic. A mule deer killed with a .280 will not know that he wasn't shot with a .270.

Yet because of such duplication or overlapping of areas of effectiveness on game, the sportsman must be more discriminating than ever before in evaluating his needs and his own capabilities (or shortcomings) before making any new addition to his arsenal. For example, an Eastern deer hunter who has no hope of making a Western mountain hunt should think twice before he buys a .338 Magnum bolt action rifle. Not that a .338 won't kill a 125 pound whitetail buck quite dead, and quickly, but this is an unwieldy rifle to lug through brush, and it carries power enough to kill a carload of such deer—if you could line them up.

The solution is to examine your needs *first*, then pick the gun that fills them best. This is simpler than it sounds if you are not misled by glowing advertising copy and the wild tales of hunters who own a new .237 Supershot Magnamus and have just made clean kills at 600 yards while balanced on one foot on the edge of an overhanging cliff. If you manage to ignore these tales, you are on firm ground.

It has always been my feeling that a man will do his best shooting with the guns that he *likes best*, authoritative opinion to the contrary. If a man has a tender feeling for a Winchester .30/30 carbine, let's say, he will kill more whitetail deer with it in timber hunting than the guy who has just bought a bolt action in the newest Magnum caliber simply because it's the latest job on the market. It must be remembered that there are fads in firearms as there are in clothing and cars. The newest thing out just might not happen to be the best item to suit your taste, physical capabilities, or personality.

Among today's American firearms there are no really bad guns; some are just better than others. It would be easy to say that you get what you pay for—but this old cliché is not entirely true. For one hunter's needs, an $80 carbine might be far more effective than a custom built job costing about $300. There is some comfort in this thought. I feel no envy at all when I run across a hunter sitting atop an Adirondack beech ridge with the latest in gun-making creations—fiddleback walnut, skipline checkering, variable power scope and all—while I am toting a .35 caliber short rifle just a bit beat up around the edges. Pick the tool for the job, I say.

To get down to cases: we have a variety of different rifle actions, and all of them have some basic advantages and some disadvantages, depending on the purpose for which they were designed and the use to which they are put. Actually, there has been little basic change in modern arms over the past 50 years, so we can look at the track record of each type.

The .22 rifles, the learning, plinking, and small game arms, are made in all actions. But the differences among them—while theoretically quite similar to

Here are the four kinds of .22s used for learning, plinking, and small game shooting: a pump action, an autoloader, a bolt action (single shot .22s are similar to this except for the clip), and a lever action.

the differences among these same actions in big calibers—are not very important. Because they transmit virtually no recoil, they are all easy to shoot; because they can be used close to home and therefore quite frequently, missing a shot with one is not the same as traveling 500 miles, tramping through the woods for a week, and missing your one and only shot at a deer. Because all .22s fire the same type of cartridge, they are all subject to the limitations of that cartridge—comparatively short range and low power. So the .22 rifle you choose is almost entirely a matter of personal preference. What we will discuss here, therefore, are the center-fire rifle actions used for big game hunting on this continent.

LEVER ACTION

Let's take the lever action design first. This is the oldest of American repeaters for big game hunting. A few "modern looking" lever actions have been made both here and abroad, but the traditional designs have remained almost unchanged since before the turn of the century. We can safely say that not much is wrong with a design that stands up that long and that well.

The advantage of the lever action gun is a fairly high rate of repeat firing,

The Browning Model BLR lever action rifle.

A classic lever action rifle, a design used since before the turn of the century. The one shown is the Marlin Model 336.

The Savage Model 99, a hammerless lever action rifle.

light weight, easy handling, reliability, and enough power for most big game at the modest ranges that cover about 90 percent of an American hunter's efforts. The lever is a middle of the road design, not as fast to operate as a pump or autoloader, somewhat faster than a bolt. It provides enough primary extraction leverage to yank out fired cases positively and, next to the bolt, is most reliable in functioning when the action is filled with water, dirt, dead leaves, or other foreign matter.

On the negative side, you will not find here the sharp, clean trigger pull of a bolt action and the ignition, or lock, time is noticeably slower than that of most bolts. In the tubular or action-contained magazine design you may find objections to the awkward insertion of cartridges through the side loading port when fingers are cold. This design also requires that cartridges be pumped through the action to unload the rifle, which means that you will need to pick them up from the ground unless you are dexterous enough to catch them as they come out.

The lever action is also a middle ground choice in calibers, since no lever model is rugged enough to take the pressures of the most powerful modern loads. In the tubular magazine types these are woods and brush rifles effective up to about 150 yards on game of deer size. However, the hammerless, rotary magazine Savage 99, chambered for .243, .308, and .358, extends this range by about 100 yards. The most modern lever is the Winchester Model 88, also hammerless and made in .243, .284, .308, and .358, with cartridges fed from a detachable box magazine to lessen the problems of loading and unloading. This modern action is rugged and is set in a one piece stock—which has some accuracy advantages over the normal two piece stock of previous lever actions.

PUMP ACTION

Somewhat faster to operate than the lever rifles is Remington's Model 760 pump, the only center-fire pump gun and a smooth working rifle that, again, carries its cartridges in a detachable box magazine. This rifle, with its ex-

The Remington Model 760 pump action, the only center-fire pump rifle.

tremely strong action, rivals some of the best bolt actions in accuracy and is made in .30/06 caliber (among others), which makes it a long range big game rifle as well as an ideal timber rifle in the carbine version, with its 18½ inch barrel. Reliability leaves nothing to be desired, though the action should be kept reasonably clean and, in cold weather, free from heavy oil.

AUTOLOADING

The autoloading guns in the big game field are three: Remington's Model 742 (which is a twin to the pump Model 760), the Winchester Model 100 (a twin to the lever 88), and the Ruger .44 Magnum carbine. This last is a brush gun, for the man who hunts deer at close range, usually the Eastern hunter in heavy timber or thicket. For this purpose it is fine, but the range

The Remington Model 742 autoloading rifle.

The Browning Automatic rifle.

The Ruger .44 Magnum carbine, a rifle designed for hunting in heavy cover.

limitation is approximately that of the old lever action carbines—about 150 yards. Each of these actions is autoloading and gas operated; the Remington and Winchester are identical with their twins in every practical feature except for manual or self-loading action. In field tests the 742 and 100 perform with accuracy to match that of the manually operated rifles—which is certainly good enough for directing hits to the vital area of big game animals at long range. In this respect you make your own decision as to whether you want to work the action by hand or have the rifle do it for you. The cautions here are that *any* self-loader is more sensitive than manually operated firearms to foreign matter in the action, ammo must be just right (hand loads sometimes fail), and below zero temperatures may cause malfunctions if too much lubrication clogs the working parts.

BOLT ACTION

The last action type, but by no means the least, is the bolt. With proven reliability in all the world's military forces for more than half a century, the bolt action stands alone in ruggedness, inherent accuracy, and maximum strength for handling the pressures of powerful modern cartridges. But it is also, by far, the slowest to operate for repeat shots in untrained hands.

The bolt action is of such simple, forthright design that little can go wrong with it. It feeds, fires, and ejects with blasé regularity under all extremes of temperature, despite bits of mud, sand, and other debris in the action. It loads readily, sometimes with a clip for fast action, and many models have a hinged floor plate to eliminate feeding rounds through the action to unload.

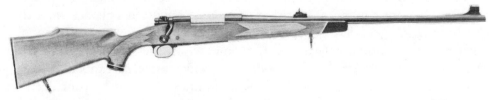

A typical bolt action center-fire rifle, in this case the Winchester Model 70.

Trigger pulls are the best to be had, and most available sporting models can readily be adjusted for trigger pull weight. Lock time is fast, ignition flawless, and stock design, on the average, is superior to that found on any of the other action types. The bolt is the rifle for the man who insists upon the maximum in accuracy with the longest range potential and greatest degree of reliability. However, bolt actions of standard design are generally longer, heavier, and not quite so "woods handy" as most of the other action types, particularly the models made in carbine length.

USE DETERMINES CHOICE

Briefly then, the choice is fairly clear. If you are a timber hunter, you probably won't choose a bolt action. If you are a prairie, plains, or high mountain hunter, you probably will. Speed in getting off the first shot and fast repeat shots in timber will dictate the desire for a short, quick handling rifle with ample power at short range; thus the short barreled lever, pump, and autoloading rifles fill the need. In long range shooting in open country, there's usually time enough for the first shot at leisure and ample time for repeat shots before the animal reaches cover, so in this category the bolt action takes over.

A compromise might be made successfully for both timber and open country hunting by choosing one of the latest models of lever, pump, or autoloader with regular length barrel, which is not usually longer than 22 inches. Not too many years ago this was considered the ideal length for a lightweight "sporter" in bolt actions, so these are really efficient arms from the viewpoint of desirable accuracy and high rate of firepower.

CALIBER SELECTION

The choice of the rifle is often tempered by the desired caliber, since a number of actions are made for a limited variety of cartridges. For example, if you want a lever action .308 you will choose between the Savage 99 and the Winchester Model 88. If you want a .30/06 pump, it must be the Remington 760. If you want the 7mm Magnum, you must choose a bolt action, either the Remington 700, Savage 110, or a Weatherby. Southpaws, incidentally, need not feel underprivileged in the bolt action class. Both Savage and Weatherby provide left-handed bolts in a wide range of calibers.

Though the action type you desire is sometimes modified by your decision as to caliber, there is much more flexibility now than existed a decade ago.

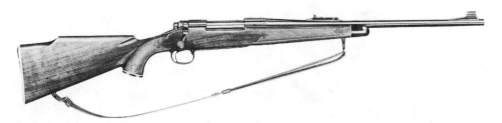

The Remington Model 700 bolt action rifle, in Custom Deluxe version here, available in 7mm Magnum and other calibers.

The Savage Model 110 bolt action rifle, also available in 7mm Magnum and other calibers. This model can be had with the bolt on the other side for left-handed shooters.

The Weatherby bolt action rifle, made in 7mm Magnum and many other calibers, offers many custom features. Among them is a left-handed bolt for southpaw shooters.

This is the famous Winchester Model 94 lever action. Though sometimes promoted as "the gun that won the West," its greatest popularity is in Eastern timber hunting.

Winchester developed the .284 cartridge, left, short enough to be used in a lever action and autoloading rifle. The .284 offers performance similar to the .270, a popular load, but the .270 is as long as the .30/06, shown at right, and lever or autoloading guns can't accommodate it.

Modern gun makers have expanded the list of big game calibers in almost every action type. A prime example is the .30/06, which for almost 50 years was available only in bolt actions (or one lever, the old Model 95 Winchester, long off the market). This caliber can now be had in both self-loading and pump action models (the two Remingtons). The popular .308 Winchester, which for all practical purposes duplicates .30/06 performance on game, is available in every action type.

The *one* best rifle for any type of hunting does not exist. Rather, several choices extend to every field, depending upon the game hunted and the type of terrain it inhabits. It is fairly easy to group different calibers of cartridges that are efficient for taking one or more species of game under specific conditions. The easy way out would be to choose the most powerful load obtainable in the desired action and let it go at that, but the problem of recoil enters the choice, and it is a significant problem.

Relatively few of our more than 15,000,000 hunters are sufficiently skilled to take the belt of an extremely big rifle without flinching. It takes experience to deliberately squeeze off the shot and place a big caliber bullet properly. Rifles in the .300 H&H Magnum class and up are too much for the average hunter to handle, even though he might be tempted because of all that extra killing power. It does make sense to pack plenty of power to kill the animal you are hunting, but not at the expense of risking a clean miss or a fluke hit which only wounds the game because you jerk the trigger in anticipation of recoil. Shooters will tell you that they don't feel the recoil when shooting at game and perhaps they don't *at that moment,* but the flinch crops up involuntarily and almost inevitably when the average hunter—who only shoots occasionally—fires a rifle of extremely large caliber.

Again, a middle course is the best. If you are an Eastern whitetail hunter, the .30/30 still does a creditable job and the recoil is mild even in a short

Here are some of the cartridges available to the big game hunter. From left to right: the .243, 6mm, .284, .264, 7mm Magnum, .300 H&H Magnum, .300 Winchester Magnum, .375 Magnum, .338 Magnum, and .458 Magnum.

barrel job. If you can take a bit more belt without discomfort (and flinch), the .35 Remington is the next step up in power. If your hunting area is Western plains and mountains, the .270 Winchester is still a top load with mild recoil. If you can handle more comeback at the butt and will hunt elk and moose, the 7mm Magnum or .30/06 is excellent.

The selection of a cartridge with ample power to kill the game you are hunting is not difficult. There are many fine loads available, ranging from the .243 to the big .375 Magnum. The .243, for example, is a sudden death deer killer with the 100 grain bullet and has little recoil. In the lighter bullet weights, it also doubles as a superb long range varmint killer. The same can be said of the 6mm Remington which carries the 100 grain bullet with ballistics similar to the .243 for deer, and rifles chambered for it will also shoot the .244 cartridges, which are fine varmint loads.

The *minimum* cartridge for mountain hunting, meaning sheep, goat, deer, elk, and black bear, should have .270 ballistics. Here you can choose from the .270, the .280, and the .284, all of which are in the same power class and allow you a wide choice in action types: bolt, auto, pump, and lever. If you can take more power and push at the rear end, you can go up to the .264 Magnum, the 7mm Magnum, or .300 H&H Magnum, all superb long range cartridges for these animals. More power than this you will not need except for the two big critters—Alaskan moose and Kodiak bear. The .300 Winchester or Weatherby Magnum, .338 Magnum, and .375 Magnum will stop these animals, and if you can take the recoil from the rifles firing any of these loads, you'll understand why. There's even one more: the .458 Magnum, a sure bear stopper, used against these animals primarily because they have been known to charge the hunter.

SHOTGUN ACTIONS

Action choices in shotguns are similar to those in rifles, except that we must forget the lever action and add the two barreled gun. Among shotgunners, the lever action is not missed. There is a shortage of American made double guns, but our market has plenty to offer in both side by side doubles and over/unders made in Europe or Japan.

For the dedicated upland shooter, nothing does as well as a double gun. For one thing, no other action type handles as quickly or balances as well. And, since there is no long receiver included in the design, a double gun's over-all length is always at least four inches shorter than a repeater's. This gives the double its noted handiness in tight cover and all-around speed in getting off a quick, unrehearsed shot. Your limit is two shots, of course, but this is not a real handicap in bird shooting. You rarely can make use of more than two while birds are still in effective killing range.

A big advantage of the two tubed gun is the ready choice of different borings: an open choke for the quick shots in heavy cover and a tighter choke for the bird out in the open or farther away. Another advantage, which is a doubtful one for upland shooting but can be useful in the duck blind, is that a double gun is faster to reload for repeat shots than a pump or autoloader. With present laws restricting the capacity of a wildfowler's gun to three shots, it is easy to see how a double gun equipped with automatic ejectors can get off half a dozen shots faster than a gunner using a repeater. It takes some time to reload those tubular magazines.

The doubles are made in two styles—with their barrels side by side or with one under the other. The difference between them is unimportant; the over/under offers a single sighting plane, somewhat easier for most shooters to use than the side by side. On the other hand, many gunners feel that the side by side is more comfortable to carry and better balanced. Many double guns do offer another choice—between one trigger that will work both barrels and separate triggers for each of the tubes. With the double triggers, the front one fires the right barrel of a side by side, the back trigger fires the left barrel. In an over/under, the front trigger fires the bottom barrel, the back trigger the top one. This makes sense because the front trigger, the one you would normally pull first, fires the barrel that has the more open choke, the one for close-in shots. After the first shot, you reach back for the trigger that fires the tighter choked barrel, the one for the farther away shots. Some single trigger guns, which normally fire the right or bottom barrel on the first pull, and then the left or upper barrel on the second, have a selection device—usually near the trigger or on the tang—that permits you to change this order of firing.

Another optional feature on some of the double guns is automatic ejectors. Upon opening the gun, empty shells are automatically kicked out, allowing

Here is one of the two types of double barreled guns, a side by side.

This is the other type of double gun, an over/under.

A pump action shotgun, this one with a ventilated sighting rib and engraved receiver.

An autoloading shotgun featuring a ventilated rib, which is not standard equipment on all guns.

you to simply insert fresh ones into the cleared chambers. This feature helps to increase speed of fire, and many shooters prefer it. Sportsmen who reload their shotshells, and who therefore want to save the used cases, don't like the ejectors for upland shooting; they prefer to take the fired cases out by hand and drop them into a pocket instead of scrambling around on the ground for them.

Aside from the double guns, you have a choice of a pump action or an autoloader. The bolt action and the single shot have extremely limited use as hunting arms, although some of the best trap guns are single shots. The pump is somewhat more rugged than the auto, which must be kept clean and must have in it factory perfect ammunition to function reliably; hand loads, if they don't conform to factory specifications, sometimes won't work an autoloader for repeat shots. In the hands of most shooters, the auto is faster, but there are experts who can work the pump faster than the auto mechanism can work itself. There are no other significant differences between these actions.

GAUGE, WEIGHT, AND BARREL LENGTH

Once you have decided on the type of shotgun that suits you best, you will be faced with the decision as to gauge, often not an easy choice in a first gun. As in selecting the proper rifle, you must think in terms of the game hunted and *where* it will be hunted. Far too many new shotgunners think only in terms of how far away they can kill the bird, rabbit, or squirrel, forgetting completely that in order to kill *any* small, moving game you must put the pattern on it while it is still within killing range.

The temptation is to buy a 12 gauge, which has been a more or less "standard" gauge since the introduction of smokeless powder in shotshells. The beginner figures this is the gauge that kills 'em far off and *he needs that*. Also, many new shooters have the firm conviction that it is a great deal easier to hit moving targets with a 12 gauge than with a 20, for example, because of a larger bore, more shot, and therefore wider pattern spread. This is not true for two reasons.

First, every shotgun (except the .410 bore) that each manufacturer produces throws the same pattern spread with the same degree of choke in all gauges. For example, a 12 gauge full choke should throw 70 percent of its pattern within a 30 inch circle at 40 yards. So will a full choke 20 gauge— or a 16 or a 28 or a 10. Pattern spreads, as far as percentages go, are alike for different gauges in guns by the same maker. There is some variation in guns of different makes and a wider variation between guns of domestic and foreign make, but all of the differences are small and of no practical significance in hunting.

Second, the actual difference in killing power among the three popular gauges, the 12, 16, and 20, firing comparable loads, is only about 10 yards—approximately five from the 12 to the 16, and roughly another five from the 16 to the 20. This 10 yard difference holds true between 12 gauge Magnums and 20 Magnums also—again, firing comparable loads. This is the only advantage of the added number of pellets in the bigger bore gun. If, for instance, the full choke 20 gauge produces enough density with ⅜6 shot to kill a duck at 40 yards (and it will), then the same pattern density will be obtained with a 16 gauge at 45 yards with the same shot size, and at 50 yards with the 12 gauge. This is based on using comparable loads in all three gauges, not a short Magnum 1½ ounce load in the 12 and a ⅞ ounce field load in the 20. Rather, each gauge, for purposes of comparison, should be loaded with its normal load: one ounce in the 20; 1⅛ ounce in the 16; 1¼ ounce in the 12.

Thus there is no really overpowering advantage to using the 12 gauge except under conditions where all the shooting will be done at fairly long range and up to the maximum possible with a shotgun—about 60 yards. The 12 gauge will always be tops for gunning wildfowl and for shooting trap, since these are long range sports. But the 12 is seen less and less than the smaller gauges in other fields of shotgunning.

The basic reason is that most shotgun shooting in the field is done at short range. Any gauge that fires one ounce of shot is an effective gauge for practically every upland and small game situation. Indeed, it was not too long ago that the "standard" hunting load for a 12 gauge was only one ounce. Today, this same quantity of shot is handled well by the 20 gauge and, in the Magnum load, by the 28 gauge.

Modern improvements in shotshell design—better powders, plastic gas seal wads, plastic sleeve protectors for the shot, and the pie crimp—produce much more uniform patterns with greater density so that a small gauge gun now does the job that only the big 12 used to. And the smaller gauge, being lighter, is quicker to handle and gets on the game faster—which is the significant factor in bird shooting.

If you want the closest approach to the one ideal gun for all shotgunning of American upland birds and small game, you would do well to choose a 20 gauge double with three inch chambers. Guns with three inch chambers are commonly called Magnums; these long chambers will take shorter (2¾ inch) cartridges, but the reverse of this is not true. In the 20 gauge, the Magnum version offers you the widest choice of loads in a gun that is acceptably light in weight. This gun will handle loads of ⅞, 1, 1⅛, 1 3/16, 1¼ ounce, all obtainable in factory ammunition. The three inch 1¼ ounce load compares favorably in performance with a 12 gauge high power, or duck, load, which will certainly make clean kills at all but the extreme ranges found in wildfowling. And this 20 gauge gun will weigh a pound less than a 12 in comparable make and model. A pound makes a big difference in your gun handling speed in the field.

The pleasures of carrying and shooting a light, small gauge gun in the field must be felt to be appreciated. At the end of a long day's tramp through brush, swamp, and over hillsides, a heavy, big bore gun becomes a real drag. If a quick chance at a flushing bird presents itself, most often your gun handling will lag and the bird will be out of range before you can get into action to intercept its flight. A light, sweet handling little 20 with 26 inch barrels will alleviate such drudgery.

A choice of barrel lengths is available in all gauges. For upland shooting, 26 inchers are best. Twenty-two inch tubes are made for a few guns, but they are a little too short. In extremely tight cover brush shooting they are all right, but such a situation is rarely met by most hunters. On the other hand, 28 inch barrels are too long and will get in the way while being carried or swung in average cover. The 30 inch barrels, the longest readily available, while they give you a longer sighting plane and their added weight makes for a more even swing, are too heavy, too long, and therefore too slow for upland hunting. These long barrels are fine for wildfowling, where you're sit-

Here are four shotguns with different barrel lengths. From the left, a 22 inch double, a 26 inch double, a 28 inch double, and a 30 inch autoloader. The last seems disproportionately longer because it is an autoloader and its receiver is longer than those of the double guns next to it.

ting down between bursts of action and not toting the gun, where a long sighting plane is an advantage for the long range shooting you'll be doing, and where a steady, comparatively studied swing is called for. Some wild-fowlers compromise between extremes by choosing 28 inchers; for trap shoot-ing, where weight isn't important but a long sighting plane and even swing are, the 30 or 32 inch length is considered best.

If we match the gun to the game—as we must—we find that the small gauges do the job on upland birds and small game far more efficiently than a 12. Even a lightweight 12 will crowd the seven pound mark, and who needs it? If I cannot kill any upland game that flies with a 5¾ or six pound gun shooting one ounce of shot, it will be my fault and not the gun's. The trick in killing these birds is in getting on them in a hurry, and this is tougher to do with a heavy gun.

At the other end of the gunning gamut is the wildfowler's smoothbore. Naturally, this is a 12 gauge gun and, since they're less expensive than double guns, you might want a pump or autoloader. This gun, which you won't have to carry around very much, should have a fair amount of weight for steady, smooth swinging and a fair length of barrel for longer sighting radius. A 7½ pound gun with 30 inch barrel is hard to beat for ducks and geese unless you are confining your efforts to pass shooting, in which case the 12 gauge Magnum is the medicine for high fliers *if* you know how to take advantage of the extra range of the heavy loads. Few shooters do.

Actually, many ducks are killed over decoys, and here you can do a good job with a smaller gauge gun, since most of your shots will be at 40 yards or less. However, there will be many chances at birds farther away than this, so the 12 is still by far the top choice in a wildfowl gun.

THE VENTILATED RIB

In any repeating style of shotgun, the ventilated sighting rib is an aid in making a quick alignment on the bird. Originally used only by the trap shooter—because of his need for more precise alignment—ribbed barrels were seldom found on any but trap guns since their weight was objectionable in guns for field shooting. However, the new aluminum alloys add an insig-nificant amount to the total weight of the gun. They are well worth this added bit of heft, especially for the skeet shooter (as well as for trap) and for all wildfowling. I like them on every shotgun, although I must admit that they aren't essential on a gun used only for upland bird work in tight cover. This kind of shooting is done so quickly that you are not conscious of the rib's presence.

The ventilated rib, in addition to helping you get on target, also dissipates heat waves caused by the ignition of a cartridge. This is of great importance to the skeet or trap marksman; he will fire many shots in a short time, and without a ventilated rib he will sight along the barrel of his gun and see heat waves coming from the muzzle. This causes mirage and makes his target extremely difficult to hit. A vent rib, however, allows the heat to escape out the sides for the length of the barrel, and doesn't disturb his sighting. Another kind of rib, the solid rib, works as a sighting aid but hasn't got the ventilations to allow the heat waves to escape. Moreover, it is a trifle heavier than the ventilated type.

THE SHOTGUN STOCK

The fit of the shotgun to the individual is vastly more important than the fit of a rifle stock. Although standard factory shotgun stocks won't differ greatly, there is enough variation in them so that you may have to look over and try a number of makes and models to your shoulder to find the one that "comes up" about right. With the comb snugged firmly against your cheek, you should be able to find the front sight perched about one-eighth inch above the breech. Slightly more than this amount does no harm, but the gun should come up so that the front sight will be noticeable above the breech. This sighting will throw the pattern a bit high and that's good for any shotgun target, whether made of feathers, fur, or clay, since you will have to cover it with the gun muzzle to score a hit.

The length of stock will be 14 inches, since this is standard. If you are short armed and thick necked, you may want to shorten this by removing the butt plate, sawing off one-fourth inch or more, then refitting the plate. Conversely, if you are the stringbean type, the length should be increased by adding a rubber recoil pad. You can make trials, at first, by putting shims under the butt plate until you get the right length, then buying a pad that will give you the total you need. If it doesn't come out right after you have surveyed the market for pads of different thicknesses, you will need to saw off some of the butt before adding the pad. This seems troublesome, and it is, but it usually will aid your shooting.

HANDGUNS

In Chapter 9 we went into some details of handgun types and how they work. Each type has its own plus and minus factors, depending upon what you consider important in speed of fire, easy carrying, safety, accuracy, and choice of caliber. In .22 rim-fire calibers the field is wide open; you can

Here is a modern single action .22 revolver, built along classic lines.

This is a double action .22 revolver, and like many of those made today, it has adjustable sights.

This is a .22 automatic; the one shown is accurate enough for target shooting.

The Smith & Wesson Model 53, a double action revolver in .22 Jet, a small center-fire cartridge.

The top pistol is Remington's single shot XP-100 bolt action, chambered for the .221 Remington Fireball cartridge. Below it is another single shot, the Thompson/Center Contender, a hammer gun whose action opens by means of a trigger guard lever; it is available in many calibers and, like the XP-100, will readily accept a scope sight.

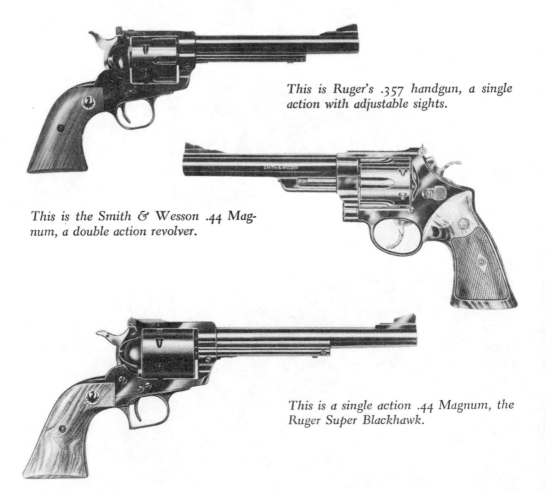

This is Ruger's .357 handgun, a single action with adjustable sights.

This is the Smith & Wesson .44 Magnum, a double action revolver.

This is a single action .44 Magnum, the Ruger Super Blackhawk.

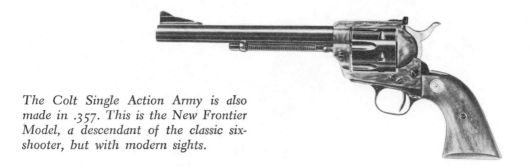

The Colt Single Action Army is also made in .357. This is the New Frontier Model, a descendant of the classic six-shooter, but with modern sights.

pick from many models in any action. In the highest power calibers you are restricted to the revolver, but this can usually be either a single action or double action.

In selecting a handgun for hunting, I much prefer a revolver for its durability and reliability under all conditions. Probably the most important factors in choosing a specific model are the sighting equipment and the quality of the trigger pull. The better these are, the better you will shoot.

The first choice for the small game hunter or plinker is a rim-fire .22. In a handgun for small varmints at long range you have the choice of the center-fire .22 Jet (in the six shot double action Model 53 revolver made by Smith & Wesson), the .256 Magnum and several .22 center-fire cartridges (in the Thompson/Center Contender) or the .221 Fireball (the XP-100 made by Remington). The last two of these guns are single shots; all three are readily adaptable to pistol scope mounting.

For big game and the bigger varmints, a good choice is the .44 Magnum, either a Smith & Wesson or a Ruger. Your decision will hinge on whether you prefer the single to the double action and whether you prefer one style of grip over the other. Either of these guns will place the bullets with equal accuracy if you can hold it.

One of these big cannons should be purchased with a long barrel and, if I had my way, I would like to see a bit *longer* barrel furnished by the two gun makers. Ruger did make me up a 10 inch Magnum and I can say that the recoil effect is noticeably less than with the 7½ inch barrel model. Neither of these guns would be used for any fancy quick draw stuff anyway, so the long barrels are not objectionable from the carrying standpoint.

Just a step down the power scale from the big .44 are the .41 Magnum, made in double action by Smith & Wesson, and the .357—made in single and double action revolvers by Colt, Ruger, and Smith & Wesson. In addition to being a hunting arm, these calibers are also used in police work although not to the extent that the .38 Special is.

In handguns, even more than in any other firearms design, you must know

The Colt Python is a double action revolver in .357 Magnum. It is one of the few handguns with a ventilated rib.

This is the standard model of the Colt .357, an exact replica, even to the grips, of a popular gun of the Old West.

Smith & Wesson makes .357s in double action; this is the Model 28.

Here is a typical defense gun, a short barreled double action .38 Special. This is the Smith & Wesson Model 12.

before you buy what you will be using the arm for and what you will expect from it. There are guns for long range varmint shooting, and they are practical for nothing else. This specialization extends to handguns for big game hunting, plinking, defense shooting, and target work.

The wide range of calibers available is one reason for this specialization. Moreover, the sights on some guns cannot be taken off; and on others the difficulty in changing them—as compared to the ease of changing and improving factory rifle sights—and the comparatively limited choice of replacement sights increase the complexity of selecting a side arm. In addition, almost every model available offers a choice of two, three, or even more barrel lengths. This, too, affects the accuracy with which the gun may be shot and the ease with which it can be carried.

GUN CARE AND CLEANING

With the introduction of modern, noncorrosive ammunition, traditionally thorough gun cleaning procedures become unnecessary. All you have to do to keep a firearm in good shape is to run a few oil impregnated patches through the bore with a cleaning rod, and go over the action and exterior metal with a clean, oil soaked rag. The rod should be inserted from the breech end, which involves removing the bolt of a bolt action gun or, for pumps, levers, and autoloading shoulder arms and handguns, taking the gun apart into its two or three major components. This is always quite simple; you'll find instructions packed with any gun you buy.

Good gun oil (which contains rust inhibitor and solvent), cleaning rods, and patches are inexpensive and available at all gun dealers.

If a gun is to be stored for a long period, coat it with a film of oil and keep it in a moisture-proof gun case or in a cabinet.

Chapter 14

HOW TO SELECT YOUR GUNSIGHTS

Today's riflemen and handgunners have it all over the shooters of just a decade ago, to say nothing of the real old-timer who had to kill his game with the most elementary sighting equipment. I am thinking of the great rash of sights, both iron and glass, now available and, in most cases, the ease with which they can be installed on modern guns.

If there is any big failing with rifles and handguns right now—as much as there was in the past—it is in the kind of sights that come with the guns when you buy them. There are two probable reasons for this: the gun manufacturer may figure that you are going to change the sights anyway after you buy the gun, or it may be that skimping on the sights makes the firearm just that much lower in price to attract a bigger market. In any case, the sights supplied on most rifles and many handguns are pretty poor examples of a modern means for directing an accurate shot.

The paradox of this situation is that many rifles today are capable of shooting minute of angle groups—keeping all the shots in a space of one inch at 100 yards—or close to it, yet they come through with coarse, poorly visible sights that can't be held within three minutes of angle by a man of average vision. Further, these sights are seldom adjustable for windage and the "adjustable" elevation system is inexact and inconvenient. To raise the rear sight, you push it up on a sliding piece of metal in which notches are cut. No one knows—or seems to care—just how much this raises the impact point of the rifle in terms of inches on the target.

In addition, the open rear sight of factory type is the poorest of all devices for aiming a rifle. The rear notches are universally too small, so that the front sight can barely be seen in dim light and it is impossible to see at all when it is pulled down into the proper position for a zero hit if the light is bad. Generally, if you check on a deer missed with open sights, you

This is a typical open iron rear sight, the type that is part of the gun when it comes from the factory.

This is a hunting peep sight, sometimes called a receiver or aperture sight.

will find that the shot went high—just another case of not getting the front sight down into the notch. Open sights also severely reduce the sighting radius of a rifle—another cause of inaccuracy—simply because the rear sight must be far enough away from the eye so that the notch can be seen at all, and this is usually at least 16 inches. This doesn't leave much distance between sights on the barrel of a modern rifle, and the situation is even worse with the popular carbines. I have a new model carbine with a distance between sights of about one foot, not much more than you'll get on a target pistol.

One way to correct the situation in a hurry is to knock the open rear sight out of its slot and fit a rugged aperture rear sight to the receiver, which is exactly what I did with the carbine I mentioned above. This at once lengthened the sighting radius to a practical distance and gave me a rear sight that I could see through quickly and shoot accurately simply by placing the front sight on the target. And that's all there is to shooting with an aperture sight, or "peep," as it is more commonly called.

There is nothing terrible about using open sights on a rifle *if* you always have good shooting light and *if* you are firing at a fairly large target at short range. But if your shooting is more precise than this, or if you are hunting on a dark day or just after dawn or near dusk, you will be handicapping yourself with these sights. There are much better sighting combinations around.

BLADE FRONT AND ADJUSTABLE OPEN REAR

The best design of open rear sight has a flat top, with a rear "U" notch large enough to be seen. Many of these sights, which have to be bought from sight manufacturers, also have a white diamond or triangle just below the sighting notch so it can be picked up easily in dim light. A number of companies also make this type of sight in semi-buckhorn or full buckhorn, meaning that they have simply added projecting ears to the flat top—which do nothing at all except cover more of the target and slow down your sighting.

For me, one of the best replacement open sights is the Williams Guide model, which has both windage and elevation adjustments in its base and a choice of either "U" or "V" interchangeable notch blade inserts. This is not a true flat top sight but has a slightly concave top surface which is quick to sight over. Also, unlike the previously mentioned sights, you can make close elevation adjustments without changing the top contour of the sight. The other types have a sliding elevator. When it becomes necessary to lower

Here is one of the open rear sights that can be installed on your rifle after you receive it from the factory. Its notch is large enough to be seen easily and the white diamond below the notch makes the sight faster to use in dim light.

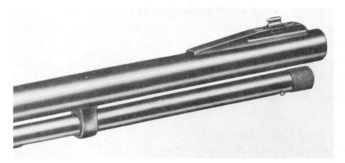

This is a typical front sight, found on a rifle when it comes from the factory.

such a sight in order to zero it in, its profile becomes a bastard type of semi-buckhorn.

The front sight is fully as important as the open rear if you are to get off a quick, accurate shot. In dim light and in heavy timber you will find that the average factory installed front sight is too small, too dull, or both, to be seen readily. The answer is a front sight that is rigged with a flat top blade of generous width (a bit more than one-sixteenth inch), topped with a white or gold insert. This is an excellent design which is lightning fast to pick up, can be seen against almost any background, in poor light, and gives sharp definition for elevation. The things that make the difference are that the angle of the insert, facing toward the sky, picks up whatever light there may be, and the flat top gives you a clear cut-off on the target for elevation. Any round bead front sight has a tendency to fade along its top edge in poor light so that you are never quite sure just where it rests against an animal target.

Generally, the front sight found on factory rifles is a compromise size that in theory should work well for shooting at small animals in open country or big animals at short to moderate range in timber. Unfortunately, this size (at or slightly less than one-sixteenth inch) is too small for quick pick up in timber and, often, too large and shiny for small targets out in the sunlight. The bright, rounded front surface of many such factory sights tends to shoot "away from the light" since the glare throws the bead off center.

You can improve this situation if you are sold on a round bead by replacing the factory sight with a half sphere (called flat face) gold bead of larger size, say three-thirty-seconds of an inch, for woods hunting. The flat face reduces the tendency to shoot away from the light and the bead is big enough to see in a hurry. If you have any gold front sight that doesn't show up as well as you might like, coat it with a drop of bright red nail polish, replacing this as necessary.

Ivory or plastic beads are not a good choice for all-around hunting sights. They are readily seen, to be sure, but are so fragile that a touch on a rock or a dead hardwood branch can crack them off.

For open country shooting, a small flat face gold bead does well. If your shooting will be in bright sun, the bright face of the bead should be smoked with a match or flame from a cigarette lighter to remove the glare. To restore the bright surface for woods hunting, just polish with steel wool.

This front sight, while it happens to be on a gun straight from the factory, is a good deal wider and more readily visible than the one in the previous picture.

Some rifles come from the factory with a hood over their front sights. These are only protectors—used during shipping to protect the blade and/or bead; you should remove it for hunting. You want all the light you can get in most instances, and the hood hinders this. Target shooters, who want to minimize outside light and regulate its intensity, always use a hooded sight, but it's not for field shooting.

APERTURE REAR

Although the majority of big game hunters are still using the open rear sight, more and more each year are coming to learn of the advantages offered by the aperture rig. This "peep," with a large hole, *never* less than one-eighth inch for hunting but sometimes as large as one-fourth inch in diameter, does two things: it eliminates any need to look *at* the rear sight to align it—you simply look *through* it at the front sight and the target—and it prevents shooting high because there is no rear notch to fill. It also gives a fuller view of the game since, as a rule, the entire animal can be seen through the peep. It also, as we pointed out, increases the sighting radius, which in itself improves accuracy.

Modern peep sights have removable discs—the part of the sight with the hole you look through. You can therefore change the size of the aperture for different shooting situations. When you take the standard one-eighth inch disc out, for instance, you have a three-sixteenths inch hole, which is fine for most hunting. You can go to the one-fourth inch size with some models or the three-sixteenths size can be reamed to one-fourth by a machinist or gunsmith.

Probably one of the best features of modern rifles is that they now come factory drilled and tapped for mounting rear peep sights (and/or scopes). The shooter, even if he is not a mechanic, can usually get a receiver sight onto his rifle without resorting to the services of a gunsmith if he follows the directions furnished with the sight. Some rifles (military and foreign models, usually) are not drilled and tapped for receiver sights so these *are* jobs for a gunsmith or skilled mechanic. In any case, the mounting of a rear peep is not the chore it was a generation ago; there is not much excuse for a man to go without this improved sighting equipment since the cost of good sights is not high.

RAMP FRONT

On many rifles, particularly military and sporting bolt actions, it will be necessary to install a higher front sight when the peep is added, as the new

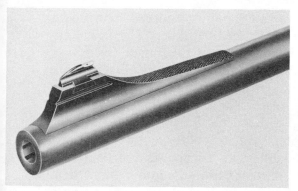

This front sight is set on a high ramp. Some rifles come from the factory with this style of sight, or you can have one installed after you get your rifle. If you put a receiver sight on your gun, a ramp front is usually necessary.

line of sight must be high enough at the rear to clear the receiver bridge, and compensating height must be added in front. The extra height necessary to zero the rifle invariably means that the front sight blade would stick up like a sore thumb and be extremely sensitive to damage, as well as difficult to find for a quick shot. The obvious solution here is to fix a ramp to the barrel and mount the sight on this. The ramp is rugged, gives pleasing outlines to the muzzle end of the barrel and tends to lead the eye up toward the front sight as the rifle is raised. Many rifles come factory equipped with ramp sights, but if your rifle does not, a ramp can be added without too much trouble. There are numerous designs for mounting, either on a barrel band or screwed and/or soldered to the barrel.

TELESCOPIC SIGHTS

We have gone into iron sights at some length because every shooter should know how to use them and how they function, and because, in many hunting situations, the front and rear iron combination is better than a hunting scope. Typical examples are deer, elk, or boar hunting in heavy timber and brush where the game is likely to be within a few yards at times and can be impossible to find quickly in the limited field of view that the scope offers, particularly in the hands of a shooter who has not had much experience with quick shooting of a scoped rifle. Another situation that calls for iron is hunting in rain or snow when, in spite of whatever you might do to prevent this, scope lenses will be obscured by moisture. This has nothing to do with internal fogging of the scope or the fogging that occurs at times when your breath happens to hit the lens as you raise the rifle on a cold day.

Nonetheless, the scope sight is the modern device for accurate bullet placement with rifle and handgun—at any range. It is, of course, a big *must* for all long range shooting on smaller game and varmints, and is a tremendous aid in big game hunting in all areas except heavy timber. The prime advantage of the scope is its one sighting device against the target; this device, the reticle, is in the same focus as the target. Furthermore, the magnification of the scope improves the view of the game and increases the size of the target area so that precise bullet placement can be made by a careful, steady shooter. Finally, the image seen through the field of view in a scope of high optical quality is always brighter than it appears to the naked eye, which means that you can do good shooting with a scope sight at both ends of the day, when the light would be too dim for you to use iron sights. Often, these times produce the most game activity, so your chances of getting a clean kill are enhanced by a good scope.

MAGNIFICATION

Since the magnification rating of a scope determines the width of the field of view seen through the tube, as well as the brightness of the image, low power scopes (2½X or 3X) are best for any situation where game may be moving in cover at fairly close range. The 40 foot wide field of a 2½X scope (at 100 yards) increases your ability to find an animal quickly in this scope before it passes from view. The better light gathering quality of a low power scope also helps you to see the game when it may be partially screened by cover. The 2½X sight comes close to the *ideal* one scope of fixed power for all American big game hunting under a wide variety of situations. It does well in timber and has enough magnification to place vital hits on big game up to 400 yards with certainty.

Scopes of 4X and higher magnification are definitely not meant for use in timber or any cover where vision is restricted. The 4X is at its best in prairie and mountain country (especially where a hunter will shoot game in *both* prairie and mountain terrain during a trip). The 6X and higher powers are strictly for high mountain terrain above timber *or* in open plains and prairie hunting for either big game or varmints at very long range.

It must be remembered that high magnification *per se* is not superior to low power. The higher the power, the more difficult it is to hold the rifle steady since your "wobble" is magnified to the same degree of the scope's power. Your actual unsteadiness may be no greater than if you were shooting iron sights, but it surely seems that way as you see the target shifting around in the field of view—all of which creates a bad psychological effect. You need a pretty firm shooting position to hold steadily on a target at long range with a scope of 6X or higher power.

These high power hunting scopes are also bulkier, because of larger lenses,

This is a typical low power variable scope, mounted on a Marlin 336 lever action.

Mounted on this Ruger Model 77 bolt action is a 6X Redfield Widefield, a scope available in several other fixed powers as well as variable power models. This telescopic sight features a wide field of view.

and are always heavier than low power ones. They are not capable of low mounting (because of their large diameter) and will change zero on rifles of heavy recoil more often than a low mounted, lightweight scope. It is doubtful, anyway, that a big game hunter really needs more magnification in a scope than 2½X—although he might think he does.

An obvious answer to the problem of which magnification to use can be solved by a variable power scope. Early models of these, with a wide range of powers, were objectionably heavy and bulky, but newer designs (with somewhat less variation in power) are no larger or heavier than conventional scopes of 4X magnification. Furthermore, these scopes have a reticle system that does not grow larger in size as the power is increased. This is of great significance when one rifle, mounted with the scope, is to be used on a wide range of game in both open and timber areas. Obviously, the scope reticle should appear fine, so as not to obscure a small animal at long range when the sight is set at the high power. Then, in timber shooting, the reticle should appear heavy for quick sighting against dark backgrounds, with the scope used at the low power setting. With most of the modern variables, you get these plus factors, but with some of the older ones you do not. In these older scopes the crosshairs (or post) appear heavy or thick at high power, extremely thin at low power—exactly the reverse of the most desirable condition.

Types of reticles vary from crosshairs to a post. Hairs are made in different thicknesses—fine for varmint shooting, coarse for big game hunting. Dot reticles can also be had in various diameters for the same purpose. However, the best all-around type is the comparatively new dual crosshairs, which appear as fairly heavy posts from the rim of your field of view inward most of the way and then become fine cross wires at the center so that plenty of target can be seen and precision of aim can be achieved. Called Dual X by Weaver, Duplex by Leupold, and 4-Plex by Redfield, this type is heavy enough for you to see it easily in timber but fine enough at the center so as not to cover a woodchuck at 300 yards. Posts are good for timber hunting, but not so good for long range shooting when your hold-over will cover up your target. For self-evident reasons, the dual wire type of reticle is also best for shooting at running game. Dots are not bad but can be hard to find quickly in dim light with a confusing background, since the wires (or spider web) on which they are mounted are so fine as to be almost invisible.

Here is a typical rim-fire scope installed on a .22 Browning autoloader.

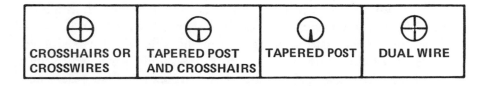

| CROSSHAIRS OR CROSSWIRES | TAPERED POST AND CROSSHAIRS | TAPERED POST | DUAL WIRE |

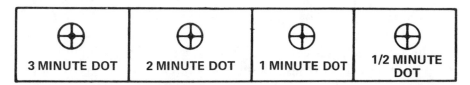

| 3 MINUTE DOT | 2 MINUTE DOT | 1 MINUTE DOT | 1/2 MINUTE DOT |

These are drawings of the various types of reticles available in telescopic sights. The dot sizes vary; for each minute of angle, one inch of the target is covered by the dot at 100 yards.

These three scopes are variable power Leupold models. The top one can be adjusted to any magnification from one (meaning no magnification) to four (meaning four times up). The one at center can be set from 2X to 7X, while the scope at bottom goes from 3X to 9X.

SCOPE MOUNTS

Mounts come in a wide range of styles for different purposes. Generally, when a shooter becomes accustomed to the scope sight, he is reluctant to use any of the iron varieties. If he has this strong a preference, he can mount his scope in a fixed position on the top of his rifle. For this shooter using this rig, it is a scope sight or no shooting. He should permanently fix the scope to his rifle with one of the many rugged top mounts that place the scope low for quick sighting and offer maximum use of the comb height of the stock. This set-up is just about as fast to use as a good pair of iron sights.

On the other hand, many hunters have the notion that a scope should be mounted so that the iron sights can also be used, by sighting under the scope. This combination is neither fish nor fowl, since a scope mounted high enough to clear iron sights is just too high to be very efficient. Then, when the occasion does arise to use the iron sights, it is almost impossible to find them under the scope for a quick shot.

One way to lick this is to use a swing-over mount that pivots out of the way, leaving the top of the rifle clear except for the iron sights. Again, this expedient is not ideal. The scope sometimes swings a bit off the mount bases and if you are not aware of this when you shoot, it is doubtful if you'll con-

Here are bases, screws, and split rings for top mounts, designed to position a scope low over the receiver so that the shooter can aim through it quickly.

These photos show the swing-over mounting system. In the first picture, the scope is in position to be sighted through; in the next picture it has been swung off to the side, allowing use of the iron sights.

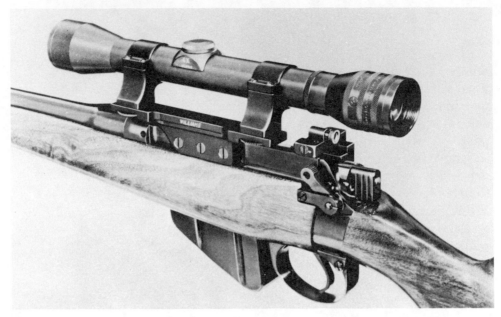

This shows the mounting system that places the scope high enough over the bore for the iron sights to be usable underneath the scope.

nect. Another point is that many of these mounts do not hold zero as well as they should and must be continually checked.

A workable solution for switching to iron sights (when weather conditions make this desirable) is to have your scope mounted in a quick detachable side mount. When the scope is removed, the top of the rifle is clean, not cluttered up with bases, so you can use the iron sights efficiently. Then, when you replace the scope, it usually goes back reasonably close to exact zero, close enough for big game hunting.

Another mounting system is available for guns that eject cartridges straight up out of the top of the receiver, notably Winchester's Model 94 carbine. For these rifles, you can offset mount a scope—that is, mount it so that it is not directly over the barrel but off to the left. Understandably, this is somewhat awkward for most shooters to use, and therefore slow to sight through. Another solution for sighting the top ejection arms is the muzzle mount, made only by Bushnell for its Phantom scope. This rig is placed directly over the *barrel* of the gun, way out toward the muzzle. It is a low power scope, just 1.3X, and is more for clarification of the target and the utilization of a single sighting device (the crosshairs) than for magnification. A somewhat similar set-up is the Leupold 2X which is mounted just forward of the Model 94 Winchester's receiver.

HANDGUN SIGHTS

Relatively few handgunners bother to make changes in their sights, since most of the side arms have permanently attached devices for sighting. The usual set-up is a square topped front sight (looking at it from the rear) and matching square notched rear, both in black. The latter is sometimes adjustable for windage and elevation. Fixed sights (that is, not adjustable) are comprised of a narrow front blade and either a rather narrow rear groove cut into the frame of the gun on a square notched rear that is stationary. These sighting devices are a part of the gun and leave little room for improvement by the shooter.

But there is some latitude in making changes to improve sight visibility for field and hunting use on handguns with adjustable sights. These arms are primarily meant for target shooting; thus, the sights are dead black to give a good clear picture against the white target paper, with the black bull's-eye resting on top in the six o'clock hold. Unfortunately, these sights are not easy to see under many hunting conditions, so it is practical to make changes. A combination of square top red bead at the front with a rear notch having a white outline is hard to beat. You will find replacement sights of this type in most sporting goods shops catering to shooters, but the changing job should usually be done by a gunsmith. Smith & Wesson guns, however, have these sights on many factory models.

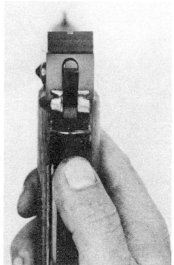

The side view of the revolver shows typical adjustable handgun sights. The view from the rear—of an automatic in this case—shows the square notched rear sight; the front sight, as seen from the rear, is also square.

The ultimate in handgun sights for accurate work is, of course, the scope. Yet, so far, the glass sight for handguns is far from ideal, since the use of a scope demands a long eye relief (the distance between the eye and the lens). This sets up optical problems not easy to solve except with a scope of low power and limited field of view. However, the scope user is more or less a deliberate shooter and will take his time to get off an accurately aimed first shot. Actually, a low power scope is all that's needed on a handgun, since the

This handgun has fixed sights; the front is a blade and the rear is simply a groove cut into the frame.

The best handgun sight for hunting is the scope. While it offers little or no magnification, it does clarify the target and eliminate the need to align front and rear sighting elements and the target. With a scope, it's simply a matter of holding the crosshairs on the bullet's intended point of impact.

important benefit of scope shooting is that only one sighting device is involved. Excellent grouping of shots can be achieved with scopes of 1X, 1.3X, 1.8X, and 2X, with the latter just about tops in power for handguns.

SHOTGUN SIGHTS

As we pointed out in Chapter 8, when a shotgun is to be used with rifled slugs, it becomes, in effect, a rifle. Therefore, it does not make sense to try to use it without adding the proper sighting equipment. One of the finest combinations for any single barreled shotgun is the Williams 5D model, with big shotgun aperture mounted on the receiver (shown on page 236) and the

This is a standard shotgun; it has one bead placed near the muzzle for a sight and there is no rib of any kind mounted on the barrel.

Williams shotgun ramp on the front. Most, if not all, shotguns will require a high front sight, and this ramp comes in a variety of heights, so you should have no trouble in selecting the right one to put your shotgun on zero at the proper range—about 50 yards.

Some hunters scope their shotguns for slug shooting at big game. The same type of scope will work on a shotgun as on a handgun, because its purpose is the same—clarification of the target plus a single sighting device, crosshairs —instead of a front and rear sight. No magnification is needed at shotgun range, so a glass of 1.5X or slightly more is your best bet. Since most shotgun receivers aren't drilled and tapped for scope mounting, installation (of a telescopic sight or even a peep sight) should be done by a gunsmith.

For upland game and waterfowl, the front bead supplied with the shotgun is all the sighting equipment you need. Many guns come with a ventilated sighting rib which, as I pointed out in the previous chapter, is an aid in all shotgunning, especially trap and skeet, but is not essential for upland work.

This shotgun has the standard bead front sight, but it is mounted on a ventilated sighting rib. The rib offers an easy to see, non-glare sighting surface; its ventilations dissipate heat waves from the barrel that cause target distortion.

(The rib may come with the gun or may be bought afterward, and installed by a gunsmith.) The bead sight is generally white, red, or gold; each color has its champions—who claim their choice is the fastest to spot, regardless of light, as the gun is mounted and swung. The difference to me seems insignificant.

On trap and skeet guns, a second, rear bead, aids in aligning the barrel with the target. This bead is usually mounted about two-thirds of the way back on a sighting rib. The rear bead is half the size of the front one; you line one up behind the other to bring the muzzle into line. This device isn't of much use in hunting because a live bird doesn't give you time for deliberate alignment.

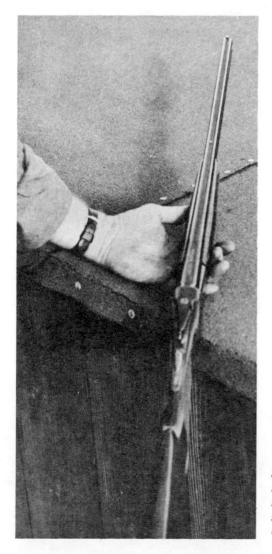

Some trap and skeet guns have two bead sights instead of the usual one. The second is half the size of the first; it is set about two-thirds of the distance back on the sighting rib from the front bead.

But you can shoulder your gun before calling "Pull!" for a clay target, and here two bead alignment helps.

Since no gun shoots better than it sights, it is a good idea to look over the factory equipment on your firearms. Almost invariably you can make improvements that will give you more one shot kills.

Like your sights, your gun handling techniques can always be improved. In this book we have told you how to master these techniques. It's time now to repeat three vital points: any normal person can become a good shot with properly guided practice; almost no one can become expert without practice; and no one is so good a marksman that he can't improve by occasionally consulting a reference work.